FACEBOOK MARKETING
MASTERY 2020:

THE ULTIMATE STEP BY STEP BEGINNER'S SOCIAL MEDIA STRATEGY GUIDE. HOW TO USE ADVERTISING AND ADS FOR GROW YOUR SMALL BUSINESS, PERSONAL BRANDING, EARN PASSIVE INCOME

Table of Contents

Introduction

Since Facebook was first created, it has become an integral part of people's lives. For most it's the social platform that they spend the most time on and have been part of the longest.

However, a lot has changed since the early days of Facebook, it's now one of the top news sources used around the world, can host a variety of post types including live videos and it features one of the most sophisticated ad networks on the entire web.

Facebook has 1.18 billion active daily users. Just let that sink in, that's 15% of the world population and it's growing every day.

So, I think it's safe to say that every single business should have a presence on this social media website. Which is the main premise of this book, to get your business making an impact on Facebook.

Marketing: After the Industrial Revolution of Eighteenth and Nineteenth hundreds of years, cutting edge industry was conceived in the United Kingdom. Notwithstanding, there was very little weight on marketing. The makers used to deliver enough items for the individuals and practically the majority of that was expended absent much trouble. There was little centered on marketing as no need was felt for it around then. Being that as it may, in the cutting-edge world, every single item is produced by various organizations over the world. Furthermore, there are organizations which give a wide scope of administrations.

Hence, in the vicious challenge, it has turned out to be very basic for each organization to concentrate on marketing other than concentrating on great quality and brand picture. Furthermore, marketing can't be overlooked by any organization which needs to tap the colossal market of existing and potential customers around the globe. As of late, with the improvement of the web, various energizing methods for marketing have been created.

These incorporate meddling strategies, for example; advertising email marketing goals and less nosy ones, for example; ads on sites. They have been supported by the worldwide system of organizations which give transportation administrations of products, for example, DHL, Dimerco and so on. Ad on different sites includes posting of advertising content on various sites. Attributable to the gigantic number of web clients, which is assessed at around 2 billion clients around the world, there is a tremendous potential as far as marketing potential. Further, there has been an ascent of interpersonal interaction organizations, for example, Facebook. This idea is named Social Media marketing which utilizes such long range interpersonal communication destinations.

The fame of Facebook has been utilized by an innumerable amount of people and organizations adequately for connecting with their customers at any side of the world. According to market assesses, the present watcher ship of Facebook is at around 400 million clients and that check is expanding quickly. The marketing of different items at the prominent long-range interpersonal communication site Facebook is known as Facebook Marketing.

Facebook Marketing includes advertising in different ways. These incorporate utilization of direct advertising as standards and so forth. Facebook has propelled different advertising plans for t publicists, for example, pay per snap plans. At whatever point the notice of a promoter is clicked, it is required to pay Facebook a specific measure of expenses. In spite of the fact that Facebook charges an overwhelming expense, it is very prominent among the sponsors because of the colossal reach and the huge business openings that are received utilizing Facebook.

There are endless quantities of different applications which have been given by Facebook and have been utilized by numerous promoters around the world. Facebook would show such ads on the profile page of a client which line up with that specific client's interests, gatherings, sex or age. For instance, female clients are indicated notices of prom dresses, gems and coordinating shoes and so forth.

For a considerable length of time Google AdWords has remained the go-to online advertising stage for independent ventures, with different options regularly disregarded. Internet based life destinations like Facebook have to a great extent gone un-adapted for a considerable length of time since their dispatch. Since Facebook's first sale of stock (IPO) in 2012, the need to adapt its 1.23 billion month to month dynamic clients has turned out to be perpetually unmistakable.

Facebook advertising is intently matching the undisputed boss Google AdSense

Recently, Facebook has been increasing huge force in the online advertising space and all the more explicitly in connection to versatile advertising. In the previous year the social monster has seen 20% development in incomes from portable contrasted and Google which has seen a lot of the market fall in the course of recent years.

Facebook now offers one of the most profoundly viable advertising stages online; giving a practically interminable exhibit of socioeconomics to target: Relationship status, interests, work environment, age, sexual orientation, area and a significantly more. You are almost ensured to arrive at your intended interest group with Facebook's remarkable degree of client information.

Why advertising on Facebook bodes well today

Here are only a bunch of reasons why you can't stand to overlook Facebook advertising:

• No financial limit, it's excessively little - Get results regardless of what size your spending limit is - Facebook advertising begins at as meager as $1 every day, enabling you to arrive at 1000's of profoundly focused on prospects at a small amount of the expense of Google AdWords.

• High quality revealing - Social media is normally dubious to quantify as far as degree of profitability. Facebook advertising has fathomed that issue. Facebook offers detailing that you set to your individual needs and marketing objectives.

• A progressively unpretentious type of advertising - Facebook is an increasingly close to home, inconspicuous advertising stage; clients hope to invest energy drawing in with brands on informal communities and barely care that it's a paid advertisement.

Facebook conveys exceptionally applicable promotions dependent on our perusing history

We are progressively moving towards an increasingly "customized web" where we are given substance progressive material to our own advantages and needs.

When you visit Amazon, their landing page indicates things they definitely realize you are keen on or are probably going to purchase. Facebook has had the option to take this a stride further; utilizing its Facebook Login highlight which is now utilized by innumerable sites and administrations.

Capacity to Re-Target to prequalified customers

Facebook isn't just ready to follow our perusing propensities on one website, but over the entire of the web. This has implied that organizations are presently ready to retarget advertisements on Facebook to the individuals who have just visited their site, however didn't change over. Opening the conduits to advertising over the entire web, not simply Facebook. Specifically Facebook's presentation of its new advertising stage, Atlas expedites its standard with Google AdWords. Map book enables publicists to see offers for advertising crosswise over different sites, much like Google does. What Facebook has over Google, is that they discover considerably more about us, our interests and who we truly are.

Extra possibility of shares, likes and comments

The special reward of advertising through Facebook is the extra possibility that those you target will like, share or interface some way or another with your promotion. This enables you to go a longer distance than the advertisements you have paid for, arriving at their companions and notwithstanding circulating around the web.

Start exploiting Facebook advertising now on the off chance that you need to contend online, you have to exploit the most recent patterns and apparatuses accessible to you. Facebook does precisely this with an elite advertising stage fit to the cutting edge web.

In the event that you need to develop your online business, or you need to fabricate your image, Facebook is the perfect spot to go to and you can have excellent chances, with the notoriety that Facebook has and the a huge number of clients in this website. The Facebook advertising stage can give numerous open doors for new web advertisers.

In the event that you are new with Facebook advertising there is an apprentice's guide that you can utilize. A portion of the things in this guide are the following:

- You will be acquainted with Facebook where you will have a presentation of the "what", "why", "how", and different things identified with this social site. The basic stage you will finish will give you a grip concerning why the possibility to develop your business is so gigantic.

- You will be acquainted with Facebook advertising and see what these promotions are. You will likewise comprehend why different advertisers are on this long-range interpersonal communication site.

- You will learn and have a comprehension on why you need to utilize Facebook advertisements. You will discover that this one of a kind advertising framework is a proficient strategy for focusing on a particular statistic or a specific gathering of people who may have a specific preference for your items.

- You will likewise discover that the Facebook framework grabs data from its client's profile which you can make as your focusing on criteria for planned customers. Facebook advertising implies that lone individuals in your specialty field may be the individuals to see your advertisements.

- Creating a promotion on Facebook is anything but difficult to do and you will grasp it from these rules. With some data that you need and giving likewise what socioeconomics you need; you can undoubtedly make your promotions.

- You will be approached to give the URL connect that you need for your prospects to go to after they click on your advertisements. This can be your fan page, business update page, or other modified greeting pages that you need to.

- You will at that point be asked what socioeconomics you need to target. This data can be taken from client's profiles and you simply need to enter the subtleties, as on the off chance that you need to target sex, age, instruction, interests, area and different things.

- You will discover that Facebook promotions are not costly. These advertisements are similarly less in expense than the other online advertising techniques, in connection to its expense per impression or cost per snap advertising plans.

- With this guide you will know for yourself if utilizing Facebook promotions can give you extraordinary chances to develop, improve your business and on the off chance that it is extremely worth the endeavors. You will likewise have a comprehension of how extraordinary the method of focusing on individuals can be a powerful way and how it can access the large number of clients in this social media era.

Ready to reap the benefits of what is probably the most powerful business tool to date? Dive in and learn everything you need to know about Facebook marketing for beginners.

Chapter 1 Who's on Facebook?

Facebook may have started as a casual network for students, however regardless, now, about everyone with a site is using it.

The base age essential is 13, and there is inspiration to believe it as is being utilized by all other age gatherings.

Facebook doesn't transparently release data on their most unmistakable age gatherings, yet an examination by Pew showed that individual to individual correspondence is most predominant with the 18-29 age gatherings. Its unmistakable quality lessens with age. It is likewise utilized by those in the 65 or more gatherings.

I can promise you that, paying little respect to what age bunch you're focusing; there will be all that anyone could need customers to go around on Facebook.

By what method Might You Market on Facebook?

Facebook has three instruments (pages, advertisements, and parties) that can be utilized by anybody. These decisions have its own one of a kind markets and they can be joined for progressively noteworthy reach for your client needs.

Pages

Facebook pages take after profiles, for affiliations, affiliations, and open figures markets.

Customers can "Like" a page, which infers they'll normally get invigorates from that page in their news channel. In any case, with the true objective to see the posts each time they are incorporated, you need to tap the choice to see posts first. Something different of significance, it's believable you won't see the updates in light of the way that Facebook needs Pages to help (consume money) presents for more prominent reach on clients.

Clients furthermore have the decision to "Like" a page anyway not tail it. (Customers moreover can seek after a couple of profiles on the off chance that they wish).

Blocks: It can be hard to get a strong balance and assembling a fan base with a page.

Advancements

Facebook offers a magnificent spotlight on publicizing.

You can make advancements centered at express geographic districts, ages, guidance levels, and even the sorts of contraptions used for checking. Facebook similarly allows customers to conceal advancements they couldn't care less for and "Like" a page proper underneath an advertisement.

Ideal conditions: Ads have mind blowing concentrating on target customers.

Burdens: Ads can get expensive, dependent upon your targets.

Get-togethers

Facebook bunches resemble talk social affairs. Anyway with additional features that show pages and profiles you can utilize these gatherings furthering your potential benefit or even make one yourself (like a course of occasions). You can make a gathering related to your industry or thing commitments as a way to deal with contact potential customers.

Good conditions: Groups are free and have raised measures of responsibility.

Weaknesses: Groups can be very dull and requesting to upkeep.

The Most Effective Method To Market With Pages

Facebook pages are the most clear and least requesting way to deal with start showcasing with Facebook.

To utilize the site is free, by and large easy to set up (at any rate in their basic structures), and incredibly versatile. There are for all intents and purposes no downsides, either. Tragically, various associations don't use Facebook to their most extreme limit, or all the more terrible, use them incapably. The principles spread out in this book will empower you to refrain from submitting those blunders.

Profile Photo and Cover Image

Your profile photograph should be your logo, essential as that. The spread picture is a substitute story. It's really dependent upon you to pick what to put here. Some utilization photographs of operators, while others utilize sumptuous HD premium photographs and put their contact data in the spread picture. Pick a photograph that will refresh your page and draw the eye of your guests.

"About" Section

The "About" area ought to be put legitimately underneath your business logo. This is your opportunity to support anybody visiting your page what your business offers.

Guarantee you put incredible data here, telling people what you're association does, for what reason you're exceptional, and other intriguing focal points. Put aside an opportunity to create this region expressly for your Facebook social event of individuals.

You can copy the substance from the "About" page of your website or blog on the off chance that you don't know what to put. Make a point to fill in most of your data under "Fundamental Info." Keep it well perfect and easygoing. An agreeable tone when in doubt works best on Facebook. You in like manner may need to put your place of work in this segment in the event that you have a physical store area.

Post Useful Information to Your Timeline

What you post to your course of events, what your put will show up in the news channels of everyone who has

"Preferred" your page, comparatively as it does when you present something all alone profile.

Thusly, ensure what you're appearing beneficial and attracts on your supporters. Take the necessary steps not to post vast updates about a similar thing, and don't post endless pointless data that doesn't take into account your devotees either.

Here are a couple of contemplations for the sorts of things you should post to your page:

Connections to articles related to your association or your industry.

Connections to your blog passages.

Coupon codes for fans to get a decent arrangement on your things.

New Thing Assertions

Make associations with your fans that they may find as profitable. Yet again, guarantee that your posts are prized. Moreover, don't post over and over consistently, with the exception of if there's an extraordinary event going on, or something new of significance to them.

Ask Your Fans Inquiries

Getting your fans to favor your page is an extraordinary strategy to mix certainty and get them to confide in you, and consider you to be an innovator in your field.

What you ask depends, all things considered, on your thing and your claim to fame, yet asking open-request as a rule accumulates the best responses.

Posing inquiries on another thing thought or undertaking, can be a not too bad technique to influence your fans that your association contemplates what they need. Getting more prominent duty on a post may moreover empower you to accomplish the most elevated purpose of the Facebook News Feed.

Do whatever it takes not to Spam

Spam is one of the quickest approaches to lose fans. If you don't effectively disturb them, yet pass on constrained time blurbs about your association, while never including anything of critical worth, by then you will encounter impressive challenges getting and keeping fans. Before you post anything, ask concerning whether it really builds the estimation of the talk. If not, don't send it.

Concentrate Your Statistics and Results

Facebook Insights offers some amazingly phenomenal request for pages. Concentrate on them. For instance, say you see a noteworthy flood in fans (or a drop off), see what you've posted starting late, and check whether you can comprehend a clarification behind the example. By at that point, post an increasingly conspicuous proportion of that sort of material (or less, in case you're losing fans).

Coordinated Advertising

Facebook publicizing gathers so much measurable information about its customers, that it has an extraordinary reputation among other online networking showcasing destinations on the web.

You can target customers reliant on for all intents and purposes anything you may find in their profiles, and moreover track your prosperity with every amount.

Advancements can be continued running on for each impression or per-click premise. Facebook exhibits to your supporters what offers are for advancements like yours, so you know whether your offer is, as per others in your industry. You similarly can set step by step following so there's no risk of blowing your money related arrangement for advertisements.

Assortments of Facebook Ads

There are various advancements you can do with Facebook. You can make progressions that direct to your Facebook page, or to a site not on Facebook. You can make advancements to push a Facebook occasion, total with a RSVP partner. You can make headways for conservative application presents and application duty.

Customers Can Hide Your Ad

Facebook used to offer the decision to "Like" any advertisement on Facebook. No more. People can "Like" a post (if it's that type) or conceal the advancement. In the wake of closing an advancement, Facebook approaches the customer to decide for what reason they couldn't have cared less for it. It's beneficial information, giving comprehension into why your advancements presumably won't do.

Change Your Ads

The extremely phenomenal thing about Facebook advertisements is that you can concentrate on advancements that can make unmistakable promotions for different gatherings. Remaining better-centered around promotions will gather better results.

For instance, you're focusing on football fans; you may make ads for various social affairs. You could have one progression explicitly accomplished for NFL fans, one at Seattle Seahawks fans, and another at Raiders fans, and a brief span later have those advancements introduced just to individuals who have showed up for football, further boosting your favorable position to admirers of those gatherings.

Of course, assume you've concentrated on people reliant on their reverence for a particular book. You could determine that book in the advancement itself, to make it bound to snatch their eye. Make assorted advancements for different books, and after that objective as necessities be.

Facebook isn't just earth shattering. It's versatile. Despite what sort of association you run, it has enough special publicizing options that you can tailor your displaying tries to oblige your association, your money related arrangement, and your time goals.

To be sure, it can set aside some chance to turn out to be progressively familiar with most of its features, anyway it's worthy, in spite of a little work on your part. Facebook still is creating at a speedy pace, and reliably it transforms into a progressively essential bit of online business with internet based life advertising.

It's moreover indispensable to capitalize on current chances. For the event, organizations that are insightful about Facebook advertisements still value an early-adopter advantage.

Once more standard sponsors start advancing into space, competition will manufacture, publicizing costs will rise, and customers will end up being much pickier. In case Facebook is unquestionably not a present bit of your promoting exertion, it should be. Set aside some an opportunity to pick up a chance to develop your business, start a few promotions, and see what occurs.

Every one of these procedures work in Facebook, however you simply need to become acclimated to rehearsing how things work, when you do it, at that point it turns out to be anything but difficult to do, your business will soar.

Chapter 2 An Overview of Facebook Marketing

Facebook is one of the largest social network platforms in the world with at least more than 1.30 billion active users, meaning that about 62% of users log into Facebook daily, a fact that makes it such a dynamic marketing platform. According to eMarketer, about 41% of US small businesses use Facebook as part of their online marketing strategy. The momentum with which Facebook has grown right from its launch a few years ago to where it is today only shows that it will likely experience continual growth in the future. Having such a large user base makes it a great selling platform, and ignoring it isn't an option for serious marketers.

Even with the widespread use of Facebook for marketing purposes, only about 45% of business owners have reported success with their Facebook marketing efforts, according to a survey carried out by Social Media Examiner. Business owners therefore need to understand the strategies and practices capable of granting them a positive return on investment that's worth the effort. Understanding the major components of Facebook marketing is vital to equip business owners with best practices and actionable insights that, if properly implemented, have the potential of giving the desired results.

Every day, Facebook presents entrepreneurs with a market for their products and services, and the question arises as to how one can target such a huge user base. Facebook has made it easy for marketers to establish an advertising platform and specify the type of people they want to target with their strategies. Marketers can target the right market using location of users, as well as interests and demographics. Understanding how you can use Facebook marketing to your advantage is quite vital for the success of a business.

Facebook started as a social network platform for college students, but has so far evolved into a platform that anyone with an Internet connection can access. The minimum age required for users is just 13 years, which covers a wide base of users, and it is being used by people of all ages. Facebook is popularly used by those between 18 and 65; however, the above and below age groups tend to minimally engage with the platform. Regardless of the age group you're targeting, you will find more than enough users to interact with on Facebook.

Engaging in Facebook marketing can help you realize may things:

- Strengthen brand identity

- Collect feedback from customers and build customer relationships

- Direct customers to your website

- Ability to be found by those looking for your products

- Create targeted advertising for promoting your business

- Generate word of mouth advertising

- Establish and demonstrate your expertise

How to Market on Facebook

There are three tools that marketers can use for marketing on Facebook. These tools are Facebook pages, Facebook ads and Facebook Groups. Each of the tools has a way to be used and often varies; however, all can be used together for greater reach of the targeted market.

Pages

Facebook page is similar to a profile; however, it's mostly used by organizations, businesses and public figures. Users get to "like" the page which then automatically enables them to receive updates from it into their newsfeeds. Unlike profiles that require mutual friendships, pages can be liked by anybody. Pages also don't have any restriction on the number of people who can like the page unlike profiles that are limited to 5,000 people. Pages are quite easy to set up; but building a fun base or a team of committed customers can be quite a challenge.

Ads

This is a targeted advertising platform marketers can use to create ads that target specific geographic areas; they can be filtered in terms of education levels, age and the type of devices used for browsing. Users are free to close ads they don't like and can "like" the page just below the advertisement. Ads are designed with powerful parameters that are quite ideal for targeting:

the only downside is that they can be a bit expensive depending on one's goal.

Groups

Facebook groups are akin to discussion forums but have additional features similar to profiles and pages. You can create a group related to your area of business or industry, enabling you to connect with potential customers. Groups are free to use and allow for high levels of engagement. The challenge is that they can be quite time consuming.

There are various marketing strategies that can be used on Facebook; however, focusing on what is less expensive has the potential of bringing greater returns and is thus quite beneficial for business purposes. Inbound marketing is one of the ways that tends to yield great returns if well executed. It entails engaging with your audience in a way they find relatable and helpful. It involves getting to know customer goals and collaborating with them as you help them overcome the challenges they face. The best way to execute this strategy is by being available where your audience spends time - which is Facebook.

The tools available for marketers on Facebook cater to those willing to form relationships with their audience. Marketers should be able to create and distribute content that their audience finds valuable and helpful. Quality content enables marketers to connect with consumers interested in the services offered or their brands. Pushing content that your audience is not interested in can be perceived as annoying, spammy or even deceiving. Facebook marketing requires a long-term commitment and consistency in delivering quality content.

To succeed in Facebook marketing, one should clearly distinguish between Facebook advertising and Facebook marketing. As much as your Facebook marketing strategy may incorporate Facebook advertising, your strategy should also involve building engaging and lasting relationships with your audience. The content you share should not always be geared towards making a sale or pitching a product; connecting and providing helpful information to your social network can go a long way toward providing long-term reliable customers you can engage with.

You don't need a big budget to get started and be successful at Facebook marketing; commitment to providing valuable content in a reliable and consistent way can greatly help in connecting with potential customers and fans. All you have to do as you start out is to ensure that you highlight your brand values in a clear and effective way, identify your audience and their demographics, while also creating a unique space for your company. Remember that when it comes to Facebook marketing, sometimes the simplest form of communication can be the most powerful.

If you have a product or service that's considered to be boring, you can awe your audience by incorporating beautiful images to highlight the creative side of your brand. Take advantage of the virtual reality features provided on Facebook to enhance your content.

Developing a Facebook Marketing Strategy

Starting off with your Facebook marketing plan without having a clear strategy in place can only lead to failure, as you're likely to become overwhelmed in the process. Take time and define your marketing strategy; just going ahead and starting a Facebook page without a clear strategy may not grant you the desired results.

You should have a clear strategy on how to meet your business goals and get the most out of every investment you make on Facebook. Below are some of the strategies you can consider putting in place.

Define your Audience

Targeting the right audience effectively may not be possible if you don't know your audience well. Defining it may not be easy if you're just starting out; however, an overview of Facebook demographics and having brand intelligence about the customer profile will act as the first building block in developing an understanding of how your audience may turn out to be. You can use tools such as Facebook audience insights to investigate key details about potential customers you may find on Facebook. Details such as age, gender, relationship status, education, location, Facebook usage and past purchase activity can give you insight into how to define your audience.

Set your Goals

Having clear marketing goals is also vital. You can invest in getting more "likes" to your business page; but if the likes are not part of your broader marketing plan, then having more likes may not yield great returns. Remember the goals differ from one business to another but should be based on specific actions that will have an impact on the bottom line, actions that lead to increased conversions to your website, generating leads and improving customer service response. These may be broad marketing goals, and you can consider goals that are more specific and measurable.

Every engagement you involve yourself in, whether it is posting content, making a comment or even designing an ad, should support your business goals. You can instill all the aspects of your Facebook marketing plan by having a marketing mission statement that suits your brand. It should enable you to maintain a brand voice that is consistent in all your Facebook marketing activities. Having a goal gives the marketing process direction and is a way of measuring the success. Some of the business goals for using Facebook include:

- Find people searching for the services or products you are offering

- Connect and engage with potential and current customers

- Build a community around your business

- Promote your other content such as webinars, blog articles and the like

Create a Facebook Marketing Plan

Once you have set goals, you will then develop a clear plan on how to achieve them. One vital plan you should formulate is determining the ideal content mix for your audience. You can follow the common 80 – 20 rule. This is where 80 percent of your Facebook posts are focused on informing, educating and entertaining with the other 20 percent focused on directly promoting your brand. The key thing about Facebook you need to remember is that the engagements should be geared towards relationships, and the constant pitching of your products may not be the best way to build them.

If you're committed to providing valuable content that your followers find helpful and keeps them engaged, they will be open learning about the services or products you are offering with the 20 percent of the sales-focused posts. You can also follow the social media rule of thirds to provide a mix of promotional posts and valuable content. It entails a third of your content covering ideas and stories, a third involving personal interactions with your followers, and the remaining one-third focused on promoting your business. Regardless of the plan you choose, it should be aimed at providing more valuable content than promotional material so as to keep your audience engaged and interested.

According to Facebook algorithms, brands that focus more on driving sales often get penalized. Facebook require that users' feeds be filled with content they like and are willing to share instead of sales pitches. Remember that likes and shares help extend your reach as they puts your brand before many people without any direct effort from your side.

After defining your content mix, the next step is to determine how frequently you should post. As much as posts don't appear in their chronological order based on the algorithms, you can plan on posting at a time when your audience is more active on the platform. Establish a content calendar to help with balancing and mixing different types of content for your posting to be on track.

Chapter 3 Why Use Social Media For Business

Currently you may be selling one of the most wonderful products on the marketplace today, you could really connect as well as assist the world. Nevertheless, having the most effective item doesn't mean that individuals will be able know about it or what it is you created. You may be making no sales whatsoever. You don't have the ideal knowledge of advertising and marketing, and also this equates to no person seeing your item or what solutions you are using. To complete this, you require to recognize how to arrangement promos and also marketing campaigns.

With all that stated, you can't just advertise anywhere nowadays, publications, papers and craigslist isn't going to do it. The internet is the future, and it will certainly be a matter of time when all old approaches of promoting your service will not function, actually it does not function, with online engulfing the past, we are building business of the future with social media sites advertising and marketing. This isn't ruin as well as grief, it merely suggests out with the old as well as in with the brand-new.

There is the disagreement that the items you are offering are not distinct, as others are marketing it too, so exactly how does one go about scaling up their business in spite of the competition? That is where social networks advertising comes into play, the ones with the same products as you, are making even more cash due to the fact that these organization recognize just how to make use of platforms as well as social media sites to their benefit.

It does not matter if you are the stay at residence mommy with an on-line service, or you have a real stroll in shop, you require to create a brand name, and also online character, a visibility. And also, exactly how you do this, is with social networks advertising.

Social media site is extra prominent than ever, as well as when it involves marketing, it's a wonderful way to take your company to the next level. A lot has been stated about social media sites advertising and marketing, but allows take a look at the advantages and also advantages that Facebook can offer your organization.

Enhanced Item Recognition

When we talk of developing your brand as well as obtaining customers to enjoy your item, social media sites is the most effective device for the task; you can raise your organizations prominence and dominate the competitors in no time. And also, not only this, you will also be standing up as well as close with what consumers are looking for, what you are using, and placing you ahead of the competition.

Building Brand Name Loyalty

If you wish to remain in business for the long term, then you require to have a follower base, where customers are seeking you out as the "most likely to" for all their buying demands. Having routine sales is a wonderful perk, but with no strong base of consumers, you can promptly sink. Facebook advertising and marketing can unlock to success in your business, permitting you to obtain more in contact with customers on an individual degree, being familiar with what they desire, as well as this response can aid your service greatly. Ever ask yourself why when you stroll into Starbucks' that the barista asks for your name? This is since Howard Shultz the owner carried out a method of developing a devoted client base, by engaging them to find back as well as really feel welcome.

Expense Effectiveness

Using the old approaches of marketing your business can leave you with substantial responsibility. Social media site marketing is really inexpensive and powerful.

All you require is a desktop or laptop and also internet Wi-Fi. As your business remains to expand, it just makes good sense to cut costs, using social media sites to promote your items is a budget-friendly method.

Coming to be an Authority

Keeping the consumer satisfied as well as producing loyalty of your brand name is terrific at creating an on the internet identity for your company. You begin to get viewed as the authority on the product you are offering. This is where interaction is so essential.

With raised presence of your product throughout the various social media sites internet sites as well as involving with prospective clients, you appear much more trustworthy than other services. When others see that you are reacting to customers in a genuine means, then this possible clientele sees you as down-to-earth, and that you truly take care of the client. When you put in the effort with social networks advertisements, you have an online identity, a person that individuals look up to, and also this can result in others advertising your items indirectly for you.

Advantages of Social Media Advertising and Marketing

The advantages have actually been clear so far, if you possess an organization and haven't capitalized on social media sites, after that you need to take it to the next level. Discover how to develop profiles, get all your service information up and also ready online, create a character, a brand name, and also build a faithful client base. These approaches and also even more will certainly be showing up in the following phases in a very easy to follow format. Come to be a victor as well as pro at social networks advertising and marketing as well as Facebook ads. Dominate the competitors.

Chapter 4 Do I Need Facebook for My Business?

Around 45% of business owners, especially those in the generation of boomers and X-ers, tend to doubt the power of Facebook as a marketing platform. After all, businesses seem to have been doing just fine before the dawn of Facebook, so why is it so important to use it now? The answer lies in the fact that in recent years, there has been a major shift in culture amongst consumers.

Facebook lends a large portion of its success to the timing of its inception. At around the same time, it was introduced to the world, smartphones also started making rounds in the global community. Designed to work as handheld personal assistants, smartphones were chocked full of features that made connecting and communicating seamless and easy. In a matter of years, this brand-new technology phased out countless devices before it, including analog mobile phones, pagers, beepers, and digital handheld organizers and planners.

For most people, a smartphone would be practically useless without a Facebook app installed on it. After all, this was the main avenue for connection, giving its users unrestricted access to their friends' shared posts and updates, and allowing *real-time* communication via its Messenger feature. Basically, it let people *stay in touch* with family and friends, regardless of where in the world they might be.

Alongside the advancements in smartphone tech and Facebook, other avenues also started opening up thanks to the increasing accessibility of the internet. Now, with more people spending time on the web thanks to the convenience of their handheld devices, they were also able to browse products and services online. Soon enough, browsing would become full-on retail with the birth of e-commerce. Essentially, this allowed people to *pay online* and everything from home simply using a smartphone or Pc.

While Facebook remained largely a socializing platform, its growing base of users sparked a brand-new potential. With almost half of the world's population using Facebook, any business that used it as their stage to reach the world around them might just be able to achieve international success *via the internet alone*. And that's when the grand Facebook marketing race began.

After launching Facebook for business, hundreds of thousands of brands flocked to the platform, eager to reach the audience that it brought together from all the different parts of the globe. Here, companies would battle it out, using both organic and paid methods to reach the billions of users that Facebook brought to the table. Since then, most internet users have also claimed to *use Facebook more than any other platform when searching for products and services*.

So, how does any of this answer the question as to whether Facebook is an essential business marketing tool? Simple - *Facebook is where it's at*. If you're questioning the need for a Facebook marketing facet to your general marketing plan, remember that nearly **half of the global population** regularly uses the platform. With that, it's important to ask - *where else can a business owner reach such a wide audience in one place?* The answer is easy - **nowhere.**

But there's more to the necessity of Facebook marketing than simple conjecture. According to marketing experts, Facebook delivers the best ROI compared to any other social network currently available. They mainly attribute this to the fact that it connects businesses with the widest population across any other platform - either web-based or face to face. What's more, the use of Facebook for marketing opens a variety of avenues that could help improve how other facets of the online marketing strategy might work.

Crunching Numbers - The Statistics of Facebook Marketing

In many ways, marketing is all about numbers. Conversions, visits, engagements, reach - these are all essential marketing aspects that can be measured by way of numbers. So, if you're still not sure as to whether Facebook is an integral part of marketing in the new age, consider these high-flying digits that the website crunches out to benefit the businesses that see its potential.

Facebook sees 2.07 billion unique, active monthly users. This means that businesses could possibly reach millions (or billions, if you're that good) people every month to advertise their brand to. Compared to the performance of an average brick-and-mortar storefront that's limited to *only the population that walks that area on a daily basis*, Facebook proves to be an unmatched contender in the area of potential reach.

An estimated 77% of Facebook users have had some college education. Why is this relevant? Well, it goes without saying that the higher the education a person has achieved, the more they have to spend. With 77% of Facebook users having had some college education, a larger population also has the means to spend for products and services they might find on the platform.

Users who earn $75,000 USD or more a year have the highest adoption rate. According to statistics, individuals with an average annual income of $75,000 USD have the highest Facebook adoption rate at 76%.

There are more adults on Facebook than teens and children. So, your audience might have a greater capacity to purchase and pay online, given that most of them are working adults with their own credit cards and means for payment.

Daily Facebook users spend approximately 41 minutes of the platform every day. They've also been said to log in and out an estimated average of 8 times in a day. If you crunch the numbers, these users might see anywhere between 10-20 ads during the time they browse through the app or the desktop website.

70 million businesses are now using Facebook to interact with their audience. If you're not one of them, then you might be losing a large chunk of your prospective consumer based on your competitors who are actually making the most of the potential that Facebook offers.

The Benefits of Facebook Marketing for Beginners

Now that we've got *some* of the numbers down, it's time to talk benefits. One of the ways a business owner can appreciate the importance of Facebook marketing for a brand is by understanding the unique advantages it offers to those who seek out its potential.

What's especially ideal about Facebook is that it offers a lot of unique functions that businesses might not be able to access anywhere else, making it a truly unique platform that no other can replace.

It Lets You Connect - Before business owners could make the connection between their business and Facebook, they mostly thought that having an operational website was the pinnacle of online marketing success. As the years rolled on and marketing strategies developed, however, it became clear that run-of-the-mill websites wouldn't be able to provide one crucial factor that was unique to Facebook - direct communication with prospects and patrons.

Perhaps the closest equivalent any website could offer to match the instant messaging function that Facebook offers is the Contact Page. Even then, inquirers would have to go through the tedious process of filling out their information and waiting for a response. Chatbots - which are generally seen as inefficient and unreliable pop-up nuances - were also a failed attempt at mimicking Facebook's instant messenger.

True enough Facebook's original purpose as a *social* media platform puts it a cut above any other media a marketer might be able to use in this modern day and age. The fact that the website was designed for instant communication - a feature that rings well with consumers who want fast, easy, and convenient purchases - makes it the avenue of choice for most buyers.

Of the 70 million businesses on Facebook however, only 20 million actively use the messaging feature. Fortunately for this small fraction, their efforts pay off, garnering them a more positive online reputation and increased ROI compared to their non-messenger available competition.

It's (Mostly) Free - Despite offering companies the opportunity to connect with 2 billion people the world over, Facebook for business remains - for the most part - free. It's free to make your own business Page, free to post, and free to communicate with your prospects. Of course, if you want some of the added features like ad placements and in-depth analytics, you might have to pay a fee. But even then, most business features remain cost-free, making it a great advertising and marketing platform for businesses that don't have a lot to spend.

For this reason, Facebook marketing makes a great tool for small to medium-sized enterprises that want to reap the benefits of a full-on marketing strategy without having to shell out too much up front. As their business grows and their audience builds on the platform, they have the option to allocate a portion of their sales to pay for advertisements and other features.

It Helps Establish a Brand Personality - Your brand personality will essentially dictate the kind of consumers you reel in. Edgy, high-end brands that market their products and services as 'premium' quality will draw in high paying consumers. Those that aim for a more budget-friendly business aura will likely attract budget-conscious consumers. So, in a lot of ways, the personality of your brand might have an impact on the prices of your goods and services.

Through Facebook, it becomes easier to establish a personality because you can communicate directly with buyers. Take the case of two Facebook businesses that seem to have maximized their audience simply by way of establishing a personality that resounds well with consumers.

In one corner, we have Lexus - a premiere automobile brand that's been crowned Japan's largest-selling luxury car company. Their Facebook showcases the business's personality well, using minimalist photographs and banking less on text and more on the feeling of luxury. Communication with inquirers is relatively quick, and the air of professionalism is impeccably maintained even in the private chatroom. This aura of sophistication and class does well for the Lexus brand, keeping its reputation as a luxury car company well-maintained in the minds of those who see it on social media.

In the other corner, we have *Angkas* - a Filipino word that roughly translates to "riding on the back of a motorcycle." This ride-hailing app exclusively caters to passengers who need quick transportation that doesn't cost a lot. On Facebook, the *Angkas* app largely relies on self-depreciating humor, while jabbing lightly at its audience with passing insults here and there. It's comical to say the least, and it works wonders with the app's audience which is mainly comprised of budget-conscious students and workers who thrive on meme culture. *Angkas'* marketing specialists also goes the extra mile to respond to non-service related queries and mentions, making its Page a fun little patch of cyberspace that encourages a lot of traffic and communication.

It Lets You Repair Damage - If and when a consumer runs into a bad experience with a brand, their first instinct is to leave a bad review. Knowing full well how important positive reviews are for a business, these disgruntled buyers will often pour out their soul in the attempt to deal damage to a company that they feel might have wronged them. While some business owners might think a bad review won't do much harm, it pays to mention that 82% of prospective consumers *specifically seek out negative reviews* before deciding to push through with a purchase.

The truth of the matter is that business ownership comes hand in hand with potentially disappointing a small fraction of consumers. Hey, you really can't please everyone. But it's possible to bounce back from negative reviews if you have the right platform to address them.

Facebook allows business owners to engage with consumers in a venue that's accessible to everyone. So, if anyone leaves a negative review, you have the option to respond directly so that others can see how you handle such situations. In some cases, businesses might offer a refund, others might ask to take the matter to a private forum in order to provide a more appropriate response.

No matter what you choose to do (as long as it's pro-consumer), your Facebook audience will ultimately feel more comfortable transacting with you *despite the negative review*. Showing that you care means a lot to your buyers, and Facebook opens the opportunity for that even if in the form of a bad review or two.

It's Easy to Share - From photos, to snippets of information, to events and everything in between, a Facebook Page lets you share an unlimited amount of information with your eager audience. The platform prides itself on the versatility of its content, condensing everything that all other social media platforms do in one, media juggernaut.

Sharing on Facebook doesn't only extend your reach, but also makes it easier to keep your followers updated on your brand's latest offers, updates, and news. In fact, according to statistics, most of those who like pages for businesses on Facebook claim to do so because they want to stay updated on that specific brand's promotions.

In the same light, Facebook lets you share original, consumer-generated content. By sharing your followers' relevant posts on your page, you empower them to publish more about your brand. This fuels your positive reputation, making it easier for others to believe that you're a reliable and reputable brand.

Chapter 5 Strategies for Search Engine Optimization

Search engine optimization, or SEO, is a tactic used to boost the visibility of your website by labeling it with the important keywords in your business page that are popular with search engines. Search engine optimization will result in increased online traffic, which essentially leads to greater exposure of your site and, ultimately, to more sales. Sites that have a lot of high-quality content (i.e., text densely populated with specific keywords) can rank high without using any special techniques. However, it can take a very long time for a website to rise to prime positioning at the top of search results. SEO is how you reach that coveted spot for your business page.

Keyword Selection

Keywords are, well, key to optimizing your visibility in the eye of search engines. They consist of specific words that most closely describe the topic of your website or an individual post. You want to tune in to and focus on words that best reflect the identity of your business. For example, a nutritional business may have as its main keyword the term "nutrition," with secondary keywords of "healthy eating," "food science," and "health." Search engine software will read and analyze your page to discern if its content is rife with repeated keywords. It looks for keywords in critical areas such as the website's title, headers, metatags, and in the text of a post. It is important to use keywords that fit into your content naturally, without looking as if the keywords were simply forced into the site. If you stuff your text with keywords at random or insert keywords too close together to read naturally, the search engine may arbitrarily decide that you're trying to trick the system and it'll refuse to rank your page (clever little search engine!).

Backlink.

The second component of SEO is Backlink (BL). Let's imagine that some people are discussing nutrition in an online forum and one of the users provides a link to your website: this is called Backlink. Backlink is when other websites link to yours, allowing their visitors to also visit your site. Search engine software knows how to detect that as well. When it sees that many websites link back to yours, your Backlinks score will be higher and your website is more likely to rank higher in search results. However, the websites linking to your site must also have high-quality content for the search engine to boost your ranking. One technique some website owners try is to swap links with other websites to boost their Backlinkin score. However, backlinking must be relevant. For example, if a website about race cars backlinks to your website about nutrition, the search engine will know it's irrelevant and will not let this link boost your page ranking. And talking about a certain brand of gasoline as nutrition for your car doesn't meet the criteria! Again, this is in place to prevent website owners from trying to game the system.

If you look hard enough you can discover the techniques some people use to try to scam the search engine optimization system, but trying these techniques is only a waste of time, since most search engines are highly programmed to be able to detect what you're doing. Trying to trick, cheat, or scam the system is known as black hat SEO and your best bet is to avoid it altogether. Why risk drawing unwanted attention from the search engine algorithms and missing out on attracting many new potential customers? If you're using these tactics, then it's probably a sign that customers will think your website isn't worth visiting in the end anyway. The best strategy is to find a balance of keyword use and backlinking to supplement your engaging use of quality text, photos, videos, games or anything else you can think of that will satisfy both your customers and the search engine software. Adhering to this practice will show your customers that you're committed to providing them with high-quality content. This will result in their increased participation, which will also catch the all-seeing eye of the search engine.

Since all business pages are available for public view, your information is right there just waiting to be analyzed by major search engines. Although Facebook pages are different from original websites in that you can only build your Facebook business page from a template, as opposed to writing your own code to define it, there are still many ethical ways you can help your Facebook page rank high in results generated by the various search engines.

Optimizing Your Page Name

Your page name is the first item to address. This is what you want your potential customers to see first.

The most important place to put your main keyword is in the first word of your name.

If you are a nutritional expert who provides tips on healthy eating, your optimized page name could be something like "Nutritionist John Smith." You want your name to convey the idea of what your site will provide. Why is it so important to put your main keyword in the beginning of your name? Think of it this way: if you do an internet search for John Smith nutritionist, the search engine you use will bring you all the results for all entries for "John Smith" first, regardless of who they are or what they do. However, if you type in "nutritionist John Smith," the search engine is more likely to bring you results relevant to nutritionists named John Smith and that's what you were looking for to begin with.

Give yourself enough time to come up with a page name that conveys as closely as possible what your website will offer new customers. Although Facebook will let you change your page name a certain number of times, once you've chosen your name, stick with it. If you've chosen carefully, there should be no need to change it. Because search engines will index everything on the page under the page name, changing this essential piece of information may cost you in search visibility and possible customers.

Once you've chosen your perfect business page name, you will want to sprinkle your main keyword throughout your page, paying particular attention to the company overview section and the "about" area. Optimize your business page's short description as well; it's one of the first things your visitors will see.

Optimizing Your Custom URL

When you create a business page on Facebook, you will be given a URL that states your page name, followed by some numbers that are unique to your business. This initial URL is long, unattractive and difficult to remember. However, Facebook will allow you to create a custom URL once your page receives 25 likes. You will want to use this feature to your advantage! You won't be allowed to change your custom URL once you've picked it so choose it wisely. If possible, it should exactly match or at least come close to the URL of your actual website.

To customize your URL, you will create your "username," as Facebook calls it. Select this option and type in what you want your custom URL to be. Following the example above, your Facebook page link with a custom URL would look something like this: www.facebook.com/NutritionistJMyName.

Don't limit yourself to using only one keyword but also don't make an extensive, exhausting list either. Choose four to five important keywords that your potential customers are most likely to use to find businesses such as yours. For example, a great custom URL could be www.facebook.com/FreeNutritionTips, if part of what you're offering is free nutrition tips. Keep your custom URL short so that it is memorable, so people are less likely to forget it.

Optimizing Posts

Every time you post a text update, integrate your keywords as best and as naturally as you can, preferably within the first 18 characters. Facebook arbitrarily uses these characters as part of a post's meta tag, so you'll want to maximize keyword presence here. It can be a challenge to make your status sound as natural as possible while still including the keywords, but the effort will definitely be worth it. As you did with your business page name, try to put the most important keywords as close to the beginning as possible.

Whenever you upload a picture or a video, you can write a description to accompany it. You'll want to include your keywords here as well, in the most natural way possible. You'll also want to add a backlink directly to your company website at the end of each status update, as long as it fits naturally. You can copy and paste the link to your website directly into the status update.

Post, Post, Post!

The next step is to post as much high-quality content as often as you can! If you don't post to your page, visitors cannot see, like, or share your content, your page will be useless, and your business will suffer. Don't worry – posting often doesn't mean that you'll need to be in front of your computer or mobile device all day. Many companies hire an employee to manage their social media pages. However, even if you can't hire someone to optimize your posts, you can find automated programs that will do the work for you. I will describe these programs in greater detail a little later.

Don't forget to fill in the details about your location when you're filling in your business page information, especially if you're a brick-and-mortar business. This helps your page rank higher in search engine results when customers type your business in along with a location. Also include your phone number and hours of operation.

Even if your address is unimportant to sales, you should use the products box to provide targeted keywords. Not only is all of this information crucial for bringing your customers to your business site, but search engines also tend to rank pages with detailed information higher in searches.

Facebook Notes are an effective, but highly underutilized, tool for search engine optimization. When you post a status under your business page, Facebook will allow you to choose "write a note." The most important pieces of a note are the title and the announcement that Facebook posts to your page once you publish it (Nutritionist John Smith published a note titled Handy Hacks for Healthy Eating). You can write a note about anything related to your business and of course sprinkle in some keywords in a natural manner if you can.

More about Backlinking

The more high-quality backlinks your page has, the better your chances are of showing up at the top of search engine results. If your backlinks are of low quality, they will probably not help your ranking. For a backlink to be considered of high quality, it must come from a relevant website that has its own high-quality content and visitors must access it often. The anchor text should ideally match at least one of your keywords, and the link should ideally be included within the content and be located high on the page and not off to the side. It should be as organic as possible. The best possible scenario is when a website decides to link to your page on its own. It's also ideal if the website backlinking to your page isn't littered with other backlinks, but the few that it does have are also of high-quality. For a backlink to work properly, it must be a clickable hyperlink and not just copied and pasted text. You can insert a hyperlink into regular text. The text that serves as the base for the hyperlink is called anchor text. When you insert a hyperlink into anchor text, the text becomes clickable and will take you to the destination of the link attached to it.

Although your page will obtain organic backlinks over time, you can attempt to build backlinks yourself by reaching out to other relevant established websites and social media pages. You should think of building backlinks as a form of networking. While exchanging links with other sites will not hurt your ranking, search engines usually assume that the backlink is of high quality, particularly if your site has no backlink to the site that is linking with you.

Also, it is important to use backlinking sources that are related to your business – otherwise the search engine is likely to mark it as spamming, making it a waste of your time.

Backlink consistently. If you set up a high number of backlinks within a few days and then stop all activity, the search engines will decide that you're trying to trick the system. Since building backlinks, the right way can take time, there are services available that will build backlinks for you. Take the time to research any service owners before you commit to them. You will want to be confident that they can provide you with high quality, relevant backlinks. You'll also want to research the average cost for a backlinking service in your field of interest. Costs will definitely vary. Beware of backlinking services that offer their services at an outrageously low price. As they say, "If it looks too good to be true, it probably is. " The best way to entice a website to organically link back to your page is to provide unique and engaging content that other people will find interesting. Facebook business pages are unique in that you can host contests and write notes or post special content that otherwise wouldn't be effective on your main website. Take advantage of the features that Facebook business pages offer and use them to give other websites a good reason to backlink to you! If your main website has a blog, there is one awesome backlinking strategy you can try: copy each of your blog entries into separate Facebook notes. This is a win-win strategy because you are providing high quality content to your existing visitors and if someone who runs another website thinks your content is interesting or informative and important, there is a higher chance they will backlink to your Facebook note instead of your actual blog. Remember, search engines are smart - don't try to scam the system!

Chapter 6 Targeting your audience

Marketing and advertising are businesses in and of themselves. The idea of selling products is an age-old business that thrived long before the creation of social media. Marketing firms still exist and have traded lots of their advertising in newspapers and magazines for online ads. Still, it is necessary to have a marketing plan to capitalize on the needs of your audience and to capture your target market. Just because the medium has changed doesn't mean the content and timing need to fall by the wayside. Do your homework, find your target audience and play into their needs.

This book will read a little differently depending on the business. In general, any business is either out to sell a physical product or a service. The idea of service is very broad and could include anything from personal training in person at a brick and mortar location to providing information through a website, like a blog.

The goal for most bloggers is to put out information that is helpful and incites the desire to learn more, or change. For example, if a blogger is passionate about saving the rainforest, their primary goal will be to drive their followers to propel political change. Not every business is selling something for money, and that is a very important distinction to make. Just as well, not every business has money to spend on advertising, like a non-profit. Therefore, their marketing goals online will be much different.

The first step to a successful Facebook campaign will be discovering your target audience. Most likely, you have already started a page to promote your business. Facebook has a handy feature that will show you page statistics. Simply click on the 'Insights' tab on the top of the page toolbar. From here you can analyze each post and how well it performed. You will find stats on how many people the post reached, and how many people liked and engaged in the post. You will also find stats on how your page did as a whole through time.

The page has a list of each of your posts, how many likes and how many shares it received. What you want to pay attention to most is the organic reach. This is the amount of people who saw your post because someone they are friends with either liked or shared the page. When you think of organic, think of the growth of a thunderstorm. With the right conditions, like warm air and moisture, a giant cloud can form. With static electricity, the cloud produces lightning, thunder, and of course rain. Without these conditions, the cloud cannot form. This is your post. Like the cloud, your post must have the right combination of interest and relevance to attract followers that eventually form a cloud of Likes. On Facebook, more likes and shares lead to a bigger following, similar to the growing cloud.

Organic reach is a great indicator of interest because it shows how many people are interested in the post. The more Likes and shares mean that a post has traveled to a greater number of people in a relatively small circle, and hopefully, your target audience. A high organic reach shows that your followers liked the post, and then their friends liked the post, and so on. Use this information to develop future posts that could also grab the same attention. Organic attention is the best kind because it is essentially free advertising.

Since you have likely had an active Facebook account for a while, take some time to go through your insights and determine what posts did best, and how to build a marketing campaign from there.

Also, watch what areas of your business do best. For example, if you own a flower shop and you discover that most people are interested in your floral arrangements for weddings, play into that audience. You may find that your followers have no need for specialty balloons and other gifts, but the arrangements do well. Give your followers what they want and post more information about wedding flowers. This is good for one of two things. Your current followers will hopefully find what they are looking for in your business and provide an increase in sales, but they will also share the information with their friends and family, creating greater organic reach.

Use this information to coordinate sales and other brick and mortar marketing strategies as well. Popularity may change over time, especially during wedding season. If trends in sales can be seen online, you bet that will translate into your store as well. Test the waters and post periodically about your specialty balloons. If there is little interest and your in-store sales support that, it is likely time to rethink your inventory. Take the opportunity to pinpoint products that take up valuable shelf space and replace them with things that there is more of a demand for.

It doesn't matter what type of product you are selling; this strategy works with everything, including intellectual content which are websites and companies that do not sell a product but capitalize on information. For example, a blogger may like to post about camping. They realize that their posts on gardening and homesteading are getting much more attention lately. Topics trend and lose steam, and using page insights to determine the ebb and flow of trends can be used to your advantage. It may not be feasible to continue writing about the same topics if the interest isn't there. While many people create blogs for the fun of connecting and sharing information if you are a professional blogger who uses a website as a money making venture, keeping up with trends is valuable. Since Facebook and other social media sites are used exclusively to draw attention to these sites, gaining insight from the demographics information can be a priceless marketing tool.

Don't be afraid to ask your followers what they want. You can certainly rely on your stats and page likes to form marketing plans, but sometimes it is beneficial to be straightforward and ask your followers outright what they are looking for. This is beneficial for a number of reasons. First, you get the marketing information you are after. Second, it gives your customers the opportunity to voice their opinion and shows that your business cares and caters to the needs of its customers.

Promote your product showing its benefits and see how people respond. In your post, tell people you are considering carrying the product, and tell them you are trying to find out how to better meet their needs. Remember, most people relate better to a business that has a true human element, and most try to support local businesses when possible. Big box businesses have focus groups to tell them what products to carry. Small, local businesses have their target audience, so utilize it. Show them that you care about their opinion, and they will notice.

Try creating a simple post asking a question. Try to be specific, as the vaguer you are about the information you are requesting, the less useful the feedback will be. For example, if your business sells bicycles, ask what kind of things followers would like to learn more about. While that is sort of vague, include examples, or even multiple choice. Offer possible suggestions to prompt the conversation.

An interesting feature to Facebook Insights is "Pages to Watch." Here you can find business pages that are similar to yours and Facebook will help you compare your stats to theirs. This is useful in a number of ways. First, you can tell if a competing business has a better following than you. This can help you focus your marketing plan and will hopefully give you a boost in motivation to work harder in your business

The "Pages to Watch" feature also allows you to see post engagement for other pages for the week. Once you begin watching a page, look for sudden spikes and dips in their engagement, then compare what has been posted on their site that may have caused it. Not only can you get ideas for what is trending in your field of interest, you can see some of the advertising techniques that failed for your competition, also very beneficial information.

Let's go back to the florist example. This business owner has been monitoring their page insights but has recently been looking at their local competitors' stats as well. From their page, they determined that their specialty balloons aren't creating much interest. This created a problem in that they want to find a new product to fill the shelf space. Using a competitors' page to determine what works best for their business is a good way to find a new product that is driving business. This is very simple market research.

Regardless of your type of business, creating a solid marketing plan is vital to the success of the business overall, and overlooking social media as part of that plan is a big mistake. These tools are free online and should be taken advantage of. Creating a marketing scheme on a gut feeling will not work. Use the information at hand and make a plan that will be irreplaceable to your company.

Chapter 7 Facebook Ads Manager

For all those people who are looking to advertise on Facebook, this is a really effective marketing tool that can work wonders when it comes to creating and managing Facebook advertisements. Using this tool, you can view ads, make any required changes that you need to them, and also see the results for any Facebook campaigns or ads that you have.

Written below are a few things that you can do using Facebook Ads Manager. These are also explained in detail below.

Create ad campaigns

If you are looking to design your own ads, then this is definitely your best option. You can design your ads in a step by step process. When looking to create your own ad, you should choose the marketing objective first. Next, you should know who exactly you're looking to target. You should also be well versed with where exactly you want to show your ad and what the format of the ad should be.

Manage multiple ads at one time

Using this tool, you will much better be able to alter settings like your target audience, the budget, and the placements. You can do this on a lot of ads at one time and can duplicate your ads by creating many copies of them.

Evaluate the performance of the ads

This tool can also help you check how well the ads have performed. This is mainly done through schedule reports. This is best done by checking the results at the high-level view of the campaigns. You can also apply a lot of breakdowns so that you can check the metrics that you really want to check. After that, you can create the ad reports.

All in all, this tool is really great if you are looking to manage your ads on Facebook. It can really help you do the job in the best of ways.

On the navigational sidebar to the left are the ads, account overview, ad sets, and the campaigns. You will be able to take a quick look at those from there and will also be able to customize the columns so that you can view your results just the way that you want to.

In the modern age, your mobile device is what is with you at all times when you are on the go. This ads manager also has an application now for Android and iOS phones. Owing to the rapid pace of business expansion, it is of utmost importance for business managers to be able to manage campaigns on the go. Having said that, it is also important to mention here that there are a few features of the tool that are not available for mobile devices.

Mass Posting

Mass Posting mainly involves posting to several groups all at once. This is a feature that Facebook gives you. It makes the task of posting really easy for you since you don't have to separately post in each group that you're trying to target. You can simply mass post, and your job is done.

If you are an admin of a Facebook group and you need to mass post, then here are a few steps that you need to follow.

1. Log in to your Facebook profile

2. Next, you need to log in to your Postcron account (the Facebook auto poster tool is called Postcron.)

3. At the top right of your Facebook dashboard is the Group icon. You need to simply click that, and then you need to click on 'Group.'

4. After that, you will need to click on the group that you would like to connect.

5. Then click 'Add'.

6. After this, you will be redirected to your group settings. Once this happens, you will need to scroll to the Apps section and then clip apps. Next, select Postcron and then click 'Add' again, after which you will need to click 'Done.'

7. After you do all of this, you will need to go back to your Postcron account where you will see your connected Facebook Group.

These are a few simple steps that can really help you if you want to know how to use Facebook's Mass Post feature. This feature is really great, and it can greatly help you as a Facebook marketer. With the numerous advantages of Facebooking advertising, it is tools like these that really help and give a lot of convenience to users.

The main advantage that comes with using Postcron is that it is super simple to use and is also intuitive. This means that you can save a lot of time and energy by using it. You can even schedule your posts way ahead of time with this tool, not just on Facebook but on a lot of other platforms like Instagram, Twitter, and LinkedIn. Just imagine all the hassle that you would have to go through if you had to do all of this manually.

If you want to post to multiple groups at the same time using Postcron, then all you need to do is follow the simple steps given below.

1. First, you need to add all the groups that you have to manage using Postcron.

2. Next, you need to select the groups.

3. After that, you will have to create your posts. These can simply be text-based or with images or links.

4. Last, you need to schedule your post on the date and time that you want to post it.

In order to be able to do this, you don't necessarily have to be the admin of the group. You just need to have the Postcron App.

This is not the only application there is that helps with mass posting. If you do your own research, you can find a lot of apps that can greatly help you with it. It mainly depends on what suits you the most and the one that you find the most convenient.

Having said all of that, it is really important to mention that this feature of Facebook is really helpful and can give a lot of convenience to marketers who want to advertise on Facebook. Instead of having to go on the individual groups and then post there, they can simply mass post, and their job is done!

Creating a Facebook Page

You've caught a glimpse of the most powerful Facebook features you can use to boost your business. Among the biggest and most essential ones is a business page. Now we look at the benefits of having one.

Why do you need a Facebook Page?

In today's world, a Facebook page is essential for organizations and businesses looking to grow their online presence and reach. Below you will find the top reasons why you need one too.

Connect with your target customers.

A Facebook Page is one of the best ways to connect with your audience. It's like having a focus group that you don't necessarily have to pay for. Your audience will be expecting useful information and that's what you have to deliver. At the same time, you also get to collect useful information from your audience like their needs, pain points, expectations etc.

With the help of Facebook Insights, you get to *mine* more usable data about how they use your page and interact with your content. By interaction, feedback, and comments, they can tell you exactly what they want. You provide them an avenue to directly engage with your brand.

Through Facebook Page, you can humanize your business.

Genuine social connections are what social media is all about. With a Facebook Page, you give your business a name, a face, and a personality that people will be able to relate to. You get to represent your business but also initiate non-business interaction.

You can build a community.

In a Page, existing customers and potential customers can give reviews, testimonials and feedback. You allow them to share their opinions and voice any concerns they may have. And you can immediately address them. Building a community around your brand through a Facebook Page isn't rocket science. You can do it in many ways including the following.

- Post relevant, useful, and interesting links to articles, videos etc.

- Initiate conversations by asking your fans for comments, opinions etc.

- Encourage them to participate through promotions, giveaways and contests

- Set a section for them to leave feedback and reviews

- Provide incentive for staying active on your Page (i.e. most active member award, recognition, gift cards etc.)

It's a great way to attract new customers and build a relationship with them. If you are successful in bringing them together, you can count on a loyal following that you can keep on growing and nurturing.

You can also use your Facebook Page for Search Engine Optimization or SEO.

Creating a page isn't just a venue for you to drive traffic to your blog and website. SEO is a longer-term advertising strategy that you can maximize through your Page. Your links, posts and activities published on the Page are all indexed in search engines like Google. It can contribute to your SEO efforts and attract more traffic to your business. To achieve your SEO goals, make sure to fill your Page with rich and relevant content. These things will help improve your search engine rankings.

Make your business accessible to customers and clients every single day.

Most people log in to Facebook every day and plug in to their favorite Pages. This means it is crucial for you to regularly update your status, share videos and links as well as other pieces of valuable information. It will strengthen your connection with your customers.

To date, Facebook has over 2.2 billion active users and the number is steadily growing. There are also an increasing number of users that use Facebook to search for brands, products and services. Your presence in the platform makes it easier for them to find you. When they find you and connect with you, they are more likely to stick with you. When you manage to keep them interested and satisfied, they'd be more than happy to remain loyal and even share their connections with you.

Your competition has one.

Why should you create a Facebook Page to represent your business? Why not when your competition has one? Absence in social media leads you to miss out on opportunities. If your competitors have one and you don't, then they have a significant edge over you.

A Facebook Page is one of the most powerful and effective ways to broaden your reach. It is also a cost efficient way to increase awareness of your business. Most importantly, it allows you to build a genuine connection with your current customers, your potential customers and your fans.

How to Create a Facebook Page for Your Business?

This Page will be attached to your Facebook personal profile. It is a separate entity, it works with an independent presence and can be used effectively to promote your brand, business or any cause. There are many features available to a Page that are not accessible to personal profiles. Among them are post scheduling, advertising and analytics. To get started, here's how to create your business Page.

1. Go to your personal profile.

To begin, you have to log in to your personal Facebook profile. Once you're logged in, proceed by clicking on the **Create** button, which you will find next to your name and the **Home** button. In the window that appears, choose **Page**.

2. Enter your business information.

After clicking on Page, you will be prompted to choose between **Business or Brand** and a **Community or Public Figure**. Choose *Get Started* under Business or Brand.

You will then have to fill in the following information.

- Page Name

- Category

- Address (Street Address, City, State and Zip Code)

- Phone Number

You will be given a choice not to show the address. If you choose to tick the box, Facebook will only show that your business is within the city, state region.

3. Upload a profile picture and cover photo.

The next step is to add a profile picture that represents your business well.

An attractive image can draw attention to your page. Consider using a product photo. For instance, if you're running a restaurant, adding a delicious looking dish from your menu may be a good idea. If you're promoting a beauty salon, try using a fabulous hairstyle. Another idea is to use your business logo or any image that customers can easily associate with the business like a storefront or street sign.

The same applies for the cover photo. It has to represent the business but also be of great quality, as well as, visually appealing. To look the best, it has to be 828 by 315 pixels. Canva is one of the resources you can use for this. It allows you to create a quality image with the right dimensions. When choosing the image either for your profile picture or the cover photo, you should keep the following rules in mind.

- Pick something visually appealing.

- It should represent your business.

- It must be a high-resolution image. A profile photo should be at least 170 by 170 pixels. A cover photo should be at least 828 by 315 pixels.

Don't skimp on the images. If you have the budget, hire a photographer for product shots. You can outsource the job on websites like Fiverr or Upwork.

4. Complete your business details.

When you're done with all the steps above, Facebook will offer you tips on how to maximize the potential of newly created business page. While a visually appealing profile picture and cover photo can paint a thousand words, it is still essential that you complete the details and provide as much information as possible in order to bring life to your page.

Short Description - Tell your target audience what you are all about. This is your opportunity to humanize your brand or business. Write a quality description with smart use of keywords relevant to your industry/niche.

Keep it short and concise. As much as possible, do not exceed one to two sentences. You can describe your page's or business' focus.

Business Hours - Let your potential customers know your store opening hours.

Username – Your chosen username will be attached to your Facebook URL (facebook.com/username). Because of this, you should choose an easy and memorable one. This will help people find your page effortlessly.

Website Link – If you have one, do not forget to add your website URL. Get attention from potential customers through Facebook and drive them to your website.

Create a Group – This is definitely something you should consider. Create a section for your audience to connect with each other. It will give them a chance to talk about your business, your products and services. We will talk about this further in the next section.

5. Add call to action buttons.

If you look at the upper right hand corner of the Page, you will find the option to Add a Button. Take advantage of the traffic you're getting to prompt visitors into taking action and get the results you hope to achieve e.g. visit your website, visit your online e-commerce store etc.

Book Service - There are two options for buttons here. *Book Now* is ideal for traveling agencies, hotel or B&B's. The second button is *Start Order* which is appropriate for businesses in the food industry or any business offering products.

Get In Touch - The following five button options will direct them to various points of contact you make available.

Call Now - Let people call you without memorizing a number.

Sign Up or **Contact Us** - These buttons will direct users to your website and a form for their details. It's best for subscription capture and lead generation.

Send Message - This allows users to send you a private message through your page.

Send Email - For lengthy messages, customers can use this button to use email from the Page itself.

Learn More - Use this button to provide more information about an offer, a product or service or anything about your brand or business. There's also an option to Watch Video for people who want to see a full video post on Facebook itself or viewed from your website.

Make a Purchase or Donation - You can use this button to take them to your product page. Link it to your website. One click can take them where they need to be and purchase products or avail themselves of your services.

Download App or Game - This is best used if you're promoting or using an app to improve user experience. The Play Game button can also make your Page more interactive.

You have several options. Feel free to explore them all before you decide which is best for your business.

6. Adjust privacy and security settings.

Whether or not you're getting help in managing your business page, it's incredibly important to ensure the security of your Page. We'll look into the different settings you can customize.

General Settings

This is where you control your page. You can access the General Settings page by clicking on *Settings* located at the top right corner above the Page cover picture and next to *Help*. It should contain the below information:

Shortcuts	Page is pinned to shortcut	Edit
Page Visibility	Page Published	Edit
Visitor Posts	Anyone can publish to the page	Edit
News Feed Audience and Visibility for Posts	The ability to narrow the potential audience for News Feed and limit visibility on your posts is turned off	Edit
Messages	People can contact my Page privately	Edit
Tagging People	Only people who help manage	Edit

| | | my page can tab photos posted on it | |
| **Others this Page** | **Tagging this Page** | People and other Pages can tag my Page | Edit |

There are a couple of essential things you must do on this page and they include the following.

Shortcuts

This is about saving time by pinning your page to shortcuts section. One click from your personal profile will take you directly to the business page.

Visitor Posts

In this section, you can allow your visitors to post, add photos or publish videos to the page. At the same time, you can review the content first to make sure no inappropriate content goes through. To do this, tick the box for reviewing the posts made by others. This will give you a chance to either approve or disapprove posts before they get published.

Messages

You have to make sure that visitors are allowed to send you messages through Messenger. In fact, you should encourage them to. You can get started by checking the box for Messages.

Others Tagging This Page

Allowing individuals and businesses to share and tag the page can further expand your audience. Tick the box to allow it.

Age Restriction

If you're selling or promoting age-sensitive products like tobacco and alcohol, it is necessary to prevent minors from accessing your page.

Page Moderation and Profanity Filter

If it's important for you to keep things clean, it would be wise to edit these settings. Blocking comments containing words you may consider offensive or inappropriate will help you control published content. Do this by adding words on the prohibited section.

Similar Page Suggestions

By ticking this box, you allow the system to include your page in results of relevant searches. For instance, if you have a pet grooming business and a user searches for pet products, your page will appear as a relevant search.

Page Updates

Whenever you change or update any information from your page like a phone number or description, the system can send out notifications. It's also possible to stop Facebook from publishing those updates.

Post in Multiple Languages

If you're catering to non-English speaking audiences, you can make your page multi-lingual. This will make your page and posts appear to visitors in their local language.

Comment Ranking

Comments can be ranked so that the most recent ones or the most relevant ones appear at the top. Use this setting to indicate your preference according to what will be more beneficial to your business or brand.

Content Distribution

Your page's followers can download published videos. You can allow it or restrict it by editing this section.

Messaging Settings

When traffic volume on your page increases, it can become more challenging to manage. This is the best time to start thinking about automation.

A Response Assistant is useful in delivering automated responses to queries or any messages you receive through your page at least until you are able to respond to them. You can even customize the response to mention the name of the user who sent the message. With auto-response, you can let the sender know that the message has been received and you'll be responding yourself soon.

Page Settings

Even though Facebook Pages come with a set of tabs in default order, you can actually customize it. Pay particular attention to the tabs under the profile photo. Open to edit the settings and customize the order by clicking and dragging the tabs in the sequence you prefer. For instance, if you want to focus your strategy on videos, put that tab first.

Notification Settings

You get notified every time an activity occurs on the page. You can adjust the notification settings so you can receive them as they happen or schedule them every day. Moreover, you can choose the type of activities you want to be notified. For instance, would you like to be informed whenever your followers share your post, when you receive a comment or when someone mentions your page? You can also set to receive information through text or email or both.

Page Role Settings

This is essential if you're working with a team. Each role is assigned access to specific areas of the page. This helps clear up communication channels and delegate responsibilities among your team members.

People and Other Pages Settings

The people and pages that clicked the Like button on your page will appear here. If you ever want to ban anyone, this is where to do that.

Preferred Page Audience Settings

This is where you can specify your target audience so that the right people see your page. You can also edit this setting so they can access your posts.

7. Finalize the details.

Whenever you can, take advantage of opportunities that allow you to bring granular information pertaining to the brand or the business. Here are a few additional things you should not forget when polishing the details on your page.

- Add your other Social Media account information under Contact Info.

- To build a stronger brand and make it more personal, you may also want to consider connecting your team by linking their profiles to each other.

- Add product descriptions.

- You may also add menu.

- If you've won awards, let the public know.

After completing your page profile, save your changes and you're ready to go live and start connecting with your target audience.

Creating a Facebook Group

If you want to grow your brand or business, you would need the support of the online community. An online presence can help you stay in touch with your target audience, collect useful insights, spread the word about your business and build customer loyalty. A Facebook page will help you achieve all these. However, a group creates a more intimate and exclusive setting for your target audience to discuss among themselves and connect with each other.

What can you achieve with a Facebook Group?

- Provide ongoing updates, support and promotion to your audience who are already interested in your business and the products or services that you offer.

- Convert casual visitors to fans and then to paying customers.

- Make sure you keep your current customers happy, maintain their business and encourage loyalty.

- Always stay in touch with your business' or brand's customer base.

How to create a Facebook Group?

While you're on your way to creating your own Facebook Group, do not forget to check out existing ones. There are a couple of industry-focused groups you can learn from. They gather professionals within the industry to exchange experiences, ideas and talk about trend. They can inspire your posts that can ultimately help your business grow.

To start creating your group, follow these steps.

1. Go to your Page.

Log in to your Facebook Page, click the Create tab at the top menu bar and choose Group. This will bring up a new window where you will be asked to enter your Group details.

- Create a name for your Group. As much as possible, keep the name relevant and close to your Page's name.

- Add people to the Group.

- Include a personal note with your invite.

- Set your Group's privacy settings: closed or public.

- Pin your Group to shortcuts for easy access.

Complete the details and make all the necessary changes on your settings, then click Create.

2. Assign roles.

Your Facebook Page can be the automatic admin for the group. However, you may also want to use your personal profile as a backup admin. This will allow you to manage the Group using both your profile and your page. To do this, go to the Member's tab and click the dots that show beside your name. From the dropdown menu, choose Make Admin.

3. Add a cover photo.

Images make everything much more interesting. Personalize your Facebook Group by uploading a cover photo that best represents the group's personality.

4. Edit your Group Settings.

Complete your Group's profile by adding a category, including a description, some tags, locations, and other important details.

5. Promote your Group.

After making sure that your group profile is open and inviting, you have to start working on promoting it. To grow your community, the following strategies will help.

- Add your group's link in your correspondences with your current customers.

- Create a post about your group in all your social media accounts. Pin the post to the top of your Page so it's the first thing your visitors see. You can also tweet about it to get the word out.

- Consider boosting posts about your group.

- Invite more people who are possibly interested in the group. Make sure you customize the message of the invite.

6. Check out Group Insights.

You can learn much from Group Insights. This can be accessed from your Page. Click on Insights and Groups from the left sidebar. This will show you analytics data about your members, their demographics, comments, posts and reactions. Note however, that Group Insights only become available when you reach over 250 members so keep growing your numbers.

This is not just about collecting members for your group. It is extremely important that you keep them interested, engaged and active. Here are a few things you can do.

Regularly update your posts.

Continue generating new content that your members can discuss among themselves. Keep updating yourself about the hottest topics within your industry. Your members will appreciate your effort to keep them informed. Engage them by posting questions, surveys etc. Encourage them to add comments.

Share other content.

Don't be too self-centered. You will probably find other relevant articles worth sharing. Do not hesitate to do so. Stop selling and promoting all the time. Take a break from the sales pitch and become a genuine source of valuable information.

Explore other Facebook features.

You may also want to consider putting a face on the brand. And one of the best ways you can do this is through Facebook Live. Take the opportunity to showcase your products. You can also do Q&A or simply offer them an exclusive insight to any aspect of your business.

Keep trying different things. Through experience, you will be able to figure out what strategies work best for you. Test the waters and don't hold back. You may even want to use paid ads in order to grow your fan base.

Chapter 8 Facebook Tips to Boost Sales

A marketing strategy is essential to any ad campaign that is being run - even on Facebook. Like goals, a marketing strategy helps to keep you on track and enables you to measure your success. Without a marketing strategy, you're likely to engage in a lot of efforts that don't yield many results in the end.

When it comes to your marketing strategy, a good tip to keep in mind is that every action that you're taking in your ad campaign should be an extension of your company website. It should enhance the content that is already on your website, and it should also be relevant to the content in your campaign. The elements essentially need to flow together in a cohesive unit that makes sense for the audience.

To boost sales, you need to have goals too along with an effective marketing strategy. Your goals would depend on what you want to achieve at the time you plan to run the campaign. Enhancing acquisition of customers, delivering better customer service, creating more effective ad campaigns, your goal could be anything that you want.

Tips to Boost Your Business Sales

The one goal that every business wants though, is to boost sales. In order to do that, you need Facebook on your side. You need Facebook to be able to engage with your audience, to give them incentives to want to buy your products. Ultimately, the most effective way to boost sales is through Facebook. With that said, these tips will come in handy to help you effectively increase your sales volume and keep your business booming:

Attention Grabbing Content: Your audience needs to be interested in your content. For that to happen, your content needs to be something that grabs their attention. You are marketing your products through your website, but you need to conquer the "selling" aspect of it with finesse. Your audience doesn't want to just deal with hard selling all the time. They want you to build a connection and a rapport with them. The bond should be strong enough to get them to engage with your content. Sometimes, attention-grabbing content isn't enough if they don't feel that connection with you. To make your content stand out enough to drive sales, you should remember to include visuals, either questions or facts, be inspiring and always include a strong call to action. If all you're doing is focusing on the selling act, it is only a matter of time before your engagement will die off completely.

Don't Hold Back from Showing Off Your Products: You believed in your products enough to start a business based on selling them. So don't hold back on showing them off on your social media account either. On Facebook is where the power of suggestion is at its strongest. Using images to ignite passion, excitement, and even awaken the senses can dramatically drive your sales in ways conventional marketing methods couldn't. Create content that is going to appeal to your target audience, list down all the details that are going to get them excited and fired up, and of course, don't forget to accompany all of that with a visual that is so captivating they simply have to stop and take a second look at your ads. That is how you give your sales a boost.

Give Your Content a Boost Too: If you want to give your sales a boost, you need to first give your content a boost. Facebook has a feature called Boos Post, and it's about time every marketer started taking advantage of it. Why? Because it is effective, it's simple and easy to use, and more importantly, it *gets results*. It is also easy for marketers to measure the effectiveness of the results they get from that boosted content. Boosted posts really get your content out there in front of the audiences who matter. You can target your existing followers, their friends, and you could even target demographics specifically depending on your preference based on age, gender, and past activity.

Make Contacting You a Breeze: You've put in all that hard work to get your content seen by as many audiences as possible. Now, what you need to do is make it easy for them to reach out to you. In the old days with conventional marketing, you could reach the company through the phone number which was included on every radio, TV, and print ad that was distributed. For customers, being able to contact you is a necessity. The advertising mediums may have changed over time, but this necessity remains the same. On Facebook, your customers should be able to contact you through either Facebook Messenger, or through a phone number which must be clearly listed on your profile. With Messenger, you want to ensure that your messages feature on your profile is turned on. This allows your audience to be able to easily send you a quick message on any of their devices and ask any pertinent questions they may have. People are not keen anymore on email addresses, they prefer to reach out to you directly through an instant message on Messenger, or ring up your company if they need to speak to you directly. Needless to say, a phone number is also a must-have on your Facebook profile. No exceptions.

Run Sales Offers on Your Profile: What better way to increase sales than to give audiences an offer they simply cannot pass up? Running offers on Facebook can easily be done through your page's Publisher section, all you need to do is post the relevant details of the offer and you're set. A limited-time offer that is worth their while will make it hard for your audiences to resist taking some action. That action will ultimately lead to a sale and there you go! A boost in sales.

Using Carousel Ads: Carousel Ads are popular for a reason. They are interactive. They are intriguing. They get results. These ads allow your audience to scroll through your products and see either multiple products or multiple aspects of the same product, with a simple swipe. What's great about this ad platform is that it allows you to show groups of your products which work well together. It lets you tell a story which reminds your audience why they should be purchasing this product and how it is going to enrich their lives. Carousel Ads allow you to demonstrate a much wider range of your products, thereby giving your audiences even more reasons to click through and see what you've got to offer. If they like your products enough, you've got a sale on your hands right there.

Using Video Ads: Among one of the most powerful ad forms on Facebook is the video ad. Not only does Facebook's algorithm work to make video content a bigger priority over visuals, but statistics have shown time and time again that video content gets more engagement than any other ad form. Not only is your ad more likely to make its way into your audience's news feed thanks to the algorithm, but what they are seeing is your *most engaging* content format. Facebook's statistics reveal that audiences are a lot more likely to stop and pause their scrolling when faced with video content. Plus, showing how your products are working (showing them in action) is a great method of convincing them even more why they need these products in their life.

Bonus Tips to Get More Likes on Facebook

Because more likes equal more prospective customers, this then, in turn, leads to more sales. Therefore, part of your marketing strategy to boost sales should also include boosting the number of "Likes" you have on your business page. Use the following strategies (if you haven't already) to get your page out there in front of even more prospective audiences:

- Invite everyone you know to like your page. Literally everyone. Family, friends, long lost relatives, colleagues, ex-colleagues. Everyone you can think of. The more people you invite, the better.

- Do you have a list of prospects? Send them a quick and friendly email reminding them that you're on Facebook and why they should connect with you.

- On your website or blog, embed a social plugin for Facebook to remind anyone who visits your website to connect with you on Facebook. Offer them an incentive to like your page, like a discount voucher for their first purchase.

- Join or participate in Facebook groups where audiences are likely to have an interest in your products or services. Regularly post content on the group about your products which will help to drive and increase traffic to both your Facebook main page and your website.

- Keep track of the emails that you acquire from customers, they can be a big help in your newsletter marketing. Each newsletter should remind them to connect to your Facebook page for even more excitIng offers and reveals.

- Entice audiences to like your Facebook page by offering them a one-time discount code which they can use for their next purchase if they connect with you on Facebook.

- Engage with your followers on Facebook often so that your updates regularly appear on their newsfeed. Just because they like your profile, it doesn't automatically mean new content gets displayed on their news feed. Facebook's algorithm works to determine *which* audience see your page updates, and this algorithm is based on how closely you engage with your audience.

Bonus Tips to Boost Engagement on Facebook

Boosting engagement is also one way of boosting your sales figures. The more engaged and riveted your audience is by your content, the more likely they will be to buy from you. Having Likes on your Facebook page alone is not nearly enough to keep your business booming. You've got to make sure that they're engaged too. Engaged means that they are paying attention to your content, noticing what you're putting out there. If you've got their attention, you may just be able to persuade them to take that final step towards making a purchase. Looking for ways to increase engagement? The following strategies will help:

- Frequently engage your audience in polls to get them to answer questions. Make the topics or questions interesting enough for them to want to participate.

- Third party survey tools are great for acquiring more in-depth information. You might need to offer your audience an incentive for participating in the survey though. Some might do it more willingly. Survey Monkey is a good third-party survey tool to consider.

- Link your Facebook to your Twitter profile, it's another channel for engaging with your audience.

- Update your content frequently. Whenever there's something new on your website, update that onto your Facebook page too.

- Never neglect your Facebook comments and always make an effort to respond to your audience in a timely manner. Even if the comment is less than favorable.

- If your business has a YouTube account, don't forget to post your YouTube content on your

Facebook page too. Cross-promoting across social media platforms keeps your content interesting and engaging.

- Host frequent competitions on Facebook. Nothing gets your audience more excited than a chance to potentially win something.

- Post behind the scenes photos or photos of events that show other aspects of your brand - the more human aspect of it. Audiences like to see more than just what you're selling; they want to get to know the people behind the brand.

Chapter 9 Analyzing Results

The key to having success with Facebook ads lies with analyzing the results, making adjustments, and killing ads when they are not working. Secondly, you will want to ramp up the campaigns that are working.

Begin by identifying variations that you want to look at targeting. You can start with a general advertisement and go from there. In fact, you should include a general advertisement in your campaign in case the variations you imagine that might be required really aren't valuable. Using the example of a slot machine game, slot machines are popular in multiple countries such as the United States, Canada, Australia, Hong Kong, Japan, and the United Kingdom. At first glance, you might think that different ads need to be set up for say Japan and the United States. And sometimes this is true, but it's not always true. Sometimes you can hit on an ad creative that just works. The only way to find out is to test, test, and test.

Continuing with the slot example, we can make a single ad with our favorite video creative and then simply show it across the board. Then we can set up ad campaigns for each individual country and then run those alongside it. At the week's end, we compare results. If there is no distinct advantage to specialized ads, we can kill them. If they perform worse, we definitely kill them.

The specialized ads might work in some cases but not in others. So maybe the same ad works in Japan and the United States, but it doesn't work in Hong Kong. In that case, then you'll want to work on tailoring an ad specifically for Hong Kong.

There may be other reasons to keep your campaigns separate, but for the most part, Facebook will let you break out reports that will let you break down things by location or gender. However, one reason that you may want to keep locations separate even though they may perform the same with the same interest targeting and ad creatives is that costs are different in different countries. This also means that rewards are different in different countries. You can take this same lesson to the bank for different states and cities in the United States too.

Let's have a look at it. The cost per acquisition may be about the same if you're running the same exact ad across multiple locations. But the rewards might be different. For example, in mobile games, you earn money through ads that you show inside your game and through in-app coin purchases. Some locations might tend toward more coin purchases than others. Japan is better than Hong Kong, and the United States is where the money is (relatively speaking). However, advertisers pay different rates based on the country. They may pay a lot more in the United States than they do in say Hong Kong or France. That means that the cost of acquisition needs to be lower in those countries.

Two things you need to look at to see if your campaigns are working are:

- Cost of acquisition of a new customer

- The average lifetime value of a user

So if I have a mobile game and the cost of acquisition of a customer is $0.90 and that customer will generate $2.50 in revenue, then that is a winning proposition. However, bundling locations in ad campaigns can cause problems. For example, in the United States, an average user might cost $0.95 to acquire, but they might on average bring in $4 in earnings. In Hong

Kong, they might cost $0.85, but only bring in $1.25 in revenue.

The same thing might be in play for our real estate ad. You might easily acquire prospects from New York who are interested in moving to Arizona, maybe as easily as you're getting from people in California. But California is a lot closer, so in reality, it's a lot easier to make the move. So over time, you might find that you're making a lot more revenue from California residents but only occasional sales from New York residents. The sales from New York still add to your bottom line, so you don't necessarily want to cut them out. But maybe an approach you will take is keeping the campaigns separate and running a campaign aimed at NY residents that has a much smaller daily budget.

Testing Your Campaigns

So to review, you'll need to figure out what variations you're going to run on your campaigns. It can be varying demos, interests, or just changing up creative. The goal is to throw everything out there and then find out what works and what doesn't.

You can find out what works by running the campaigns for a week with very small budgets. In my opinion, below $3 per day is too small, but $10 a day is too large. The more you spend the more information you're going to get, but about $5 a day for a week should get you enough information to determine if a particular video or ad copy is working for you.

Data to Check on Ads Manager

You can determine whether an ad is working for you just by looking at a few parameters. The main ones to check are:

- Amount spent

- Impressions

- Clicks (or installs or page likes)

- Cost per result

You will want to know the click-through rate as well. This is simply clicks/impressions * 100. You can compare click-through rates between various ad campaigns and determine which ones are working and which ones are not working as far as generating the response to go to your site or page, to take that initial step of taking action.

Of course cost per result is an important parameter. If you are in a new business, and you really don't know the lifetime value of a customer, then you're not really going to be sure if a given cost per result is acceptable or not, however, what you can do is compare across ad campaigns to see what's working.

Now if you go to the Columns button and select Delivery, you can get the cost per 1,000 impressions of the ads. It's important to compare this cost across campaigns as well. However, note that one impression doesn't mean one person. The number of people is given by Reach. Some people might get more than one impression for whatever reason.

Another parameter to look at is Columns ??Engagement. This will let you see the cost per click. Targeting and Creative will bring many of these measures together in a single display, showing you the cost per result, cost per 1,000 impressions, click through rate, and cost per click. Even if you set up all your ads with the same exact budget – and that is what you should do – you might find some ads get a lot more impressions than others. This might happen because of demographic choices or interests that you've selected.

If an ad is really sluggish with impressions, that is telling you that you will need to open it up a bit – possibly widening the demographics, location, or adding more interests (or reducing the interests).

Killing Your Ads

After the five-day period is up, it's time to kill all the ads that are not working. Simply shut them off. This can be done by toggling the button on the far left of the listing. Keep in mind that you can turn things off at every level. So if you have multiple ad sets and ads, be mindful of what you are really shutting off.

Next Steps

The next step is the ramp-up phase. This can work in two ways, the first is mandatory. To ramp up, begin increasing your daily budget. Never increase by more than 15% per day. So we will go like this – assuming that the trial period was set to $5 Daily Budget.

- Day 1: $5,75
- Day 2: $6.61
- Day 3: $7.60
- Day 4: $8.74

- Day 5: $10.05

How high you go after this depends on how many ads your running and what kind of daily budget you can absorb. However, if you're after a large number of prospects a $10 budget probably won't cut it, and you'll need to keep increasing until you get to $40 and above. A word of warning about budget increases. For some reason, the Facebook system seems to respond better to gradual budget increases. So you aren't going to want to move from $5 to $40 or $100 in one shot. You will probably find it doesn't work. Take it gradually – soon enough you'll be at your spending goal.

Issues with bid caps

Bid caps can work in a funny way. You might find – but this depends on a huge number of factors so maybe you won't – that setting a bid cap you hardly get any traffic. In one test I did, using app installs where bid cap is replaced by an equivalent cost per install – I set a low price of 75 cents. Not much happened. I kept raising the daily budget. It finally worked – but I had to set the daily budget at $400.

That might sound scary – it isn't. At $400 the campaign was still proceeding at its glacial pace. It opened it up enough so it brought in 20-30 installs per day, and I was happy to have them at that low cost per install. This may happen to you or it may not, since there are so many factors that will influence how many impressions a given ad campaign is going to get. However, you can test the high budget if you are running into something like that which just isn't doing anything. Just keep a very close eye on it so that you can shut off the campaign if it starts spending in an out of control fashion.

Cloning

Years ago cloning showed much promise when Dolly the sheep was born. We haven't been overrun with clones, but the good news is you can clone your Facebook ad campaigns. They don't call it cloning, they call it duplicate. It's a tool that can come in handy to ramp things up. Suppose you have a campaign with a daily budget of $20 and you want to spend $100 a day, and that campaign is working really well. Instead of gradually raising the budget, you can make five copies of it and run them simultaneously. That will help you get from there to here a lot faster. It's a technique that has worked for me many times.

Chapter 10 Traffic vs. Page Likes

If you're new to Facebook advertising then you might find the types of ad campaigns a little fuzzy. We can generate traffic in a lot of different ways, you can use a lead generation campaign for example. Or you can simply use a traffic campaign that sends people to your lead generation site. Those kinds of distinctions aren't really important but the other two differ from page likes. Why would you want to use one and not the other?

Page Likes Advantages and Disadvantages

We've been through some of the advantages, but let's review them here. When you run a campaign for page likes, it's not a one-time thing. It's a connection that you're making to the client. This brings up an important point:

Use your Facebook page.

As the marketer, you don't want to just set up a Facebook page and leave it sitting there. Every time that you post on the Facebook page – it's going to show up on the feeds of people that liked your page.

In a sense, a page like is sort of like an email list. Way back when, in the early days of the internet, web marketing worked like this:

- Set up a one-page sales letter with an order button.

- Run a Google AdWords campaign that sent it traffic.

Unfortunately, two things happened. The first was Google got on its high horse and decided that it didn't like those kinds of sales pages. It wanted content, and it saw those pages as basically content free. To Google, they were evil sales pitches taking advantage of people.

Also, people began to get more skeptical. So a single sales page wasn't working as well as it had in the past.

These two developments were the birth of email marketing. The new strategy was this:

- Create a content-based website, so that Google would not "slap" you. It might include 20 pages of articles.

- Create an opt-in form on your website. People would sign up for an email newsletter in exchange for a free gift of some kind.

- Then you send the prospects a series of automated emails, giving them occasional offers to buy.

After this, things evolved again with the "landing page", which is a web page devoted to nothing more than collecting someone's email address in exchange for some kind of free gift.

Now fast forward to Facebook taking over the world. With a Facebook page, you essentially have a similar kind of setup. The Facebook page is acting as an email list, in giving you a way to communicate directly to your prospects and doing it on a regular basis.

Of course, there is no auto-responder. So you're going to have to keep your Facebook page live by routinely posting on it. When doing so you might want to occasionally slip in opportunities to buy products. If you're selling digital products, you can include a link to your sales page in a Facebook posting. You can occasionally hard sell it, but be careful with this, you don't want people to unlike your page – so only do that sparingly.

So in short, Facebook page likes to build up a customer or prospect database that you're in regular communication with. So what are the downsides?

The problem with this setup is that it's all too easy to like a posting on Facebook. So some person is scrolling through their feed, and they see your ad. Maybe it has a video they check out and they think it's cool – so they click on the like button.

But it really didn't mean all that much to them.

A large fraction of your page likes is going to be from people who aren't all that serious about spending money on your product or service. So you're going to have to get a lot of likes in order to start generating money from it. Until then, it might amount to a mere popularity contest.

Let's not get too down with this talk – having a Facebook page and getting page likes is still very useful. But don't rely on it.

Which brings us to traffic. You have a website up for whatever reason. Maybe you're selling t-shirts. Maybe you're an attorney with an informational site. Either way, your ultimate goal is getting customers on your website, not interacting with them on Facebook.

One way you can do this of course – is to post links to your site on the Facebook page. Earlier we recommended having a blog. You can integrate it with your main site, and many providers like Shopify already have a blog built-in. So you can post articles on your main site and then post them to the Facebook page.

Traffic Campaigns

However, this should work in concert with a traffic campaign. There are a couple of ways to drive traffic. Using the attorney example, you could explicitly advertise for bankruptcy services in your Facebook ad, and make it clear that clicking on the link would take a person to a page where they could contact you or sign-up on a form to be contacted.

If you are selling a digital product, then you can use Facebook advertising in roughly the same way you'd use Google AdWords. That is, the goal would be to take them to a landing page where they sign up for your email newsletter. I know, that is kind of a drag, you might have been hoping the Facebook page would help you get away from all that tedious stuff. The bottom line though is that email marketing is still the go-to technique for generating leads.

You can also do cold traffic, say to your t-shirt sight. That should be simple enough, you can have a good ad which shows the t-shirt with a sales offer. Better yet, use a carousel ad that mixes up videos of models wearing your t-shirts together with still shots of the shirt. When they click on the ad, they go right to your Shopify listing for the shirt.

Cold traffic is as risky as it ever was. However, Facebook works a lot better than using say Bing or Google AdWords, because you can show them the product in a 2-minute video before they click the link to visit your website.

Traffic vs. Page Likes

So when it comes down to it, which method is better? Chances are you're going to want to do both. While a lot of prospects that you're going to acquire from page likes are not going to be all that serious – liking a page doesn't take as much effort as signing up for emails, and your email prospects have to confirm their subscription, that second step weeds out a lot of people – the reality is a lot of people signing up for email newsletters aren't all that serious either. Think about how many promotional emails you probably get in your own inbox. How many of those do you bother opening? Probably a small fraction of them.

The best approach to marketing is to use as many avenues that you can. Page likes can be had for dirt cheap prices. So you may as well build up an audience with them. And since the old methods still work, you should also utilize traffic campaigns.

Chapter 11 Customer Analysis and Profiling

Learning about Your Customers

Understanding your customers is the key to running a successful Facebook page. It will enable you to identify key audiences, create content that will appeal to them and run more effective Facebook ad campaigns.

Customers are the lifeline of every business. Businesses that understand their customers' needs, wants and motivations clearly have a better chance of succeeding than those that don't. They are better at product development, selecting distribution channels, pricing and marketing. In order to understand your customers you need to consider the following questions:

- Who are your customers?

- What are their needs?

- Do you meet those needs?

- Are they satisfied with your product/service offering?

- How can you reach your customers?

- What will you say to them to encourage them to buy (more) from you?

According to Bain & Co, it is six to seven times more expensive to gain a new customer than to retain an existing one. Existing customers also spend 67 per cent more and after 10 purchases have referred up to seven people.

Brainstorming

Small business owners are often so busy trying to run their businesses that they haven't taken the time to consider why customers do business with them. What makes you different from your competitors? What makes you unique? You may vaguely know, but have never written it down and if pushed couldn't quickly make an 'elevator pitch', that is, in a short period of time to pitch to your ideal customer.

Brainstorming is great because there are no right or wrong answers, the idea is to write everything down. I recommend trying to make the session as informal as possible. If you are a small business with employees, invite them to take 30 minutes out of their day, bring in some coffee and pastries and let the creative juices flow! If you're a solopreneur why not sit down with a friend, partner or someone who knows you and your business?

Feedback may not be instant, but that's okay. Allow people time to warm up and encourage participation by acknowledging every suggestion and writing it down.

Here are some questions to consider using:

- When people hear what you do, what questions do they ask?

- What does your ideal customer complain about?

- What problems do you solve?

- What needs do your products/services meet?

- Think about three of your most loyal customers and consider why they like doing business with you.

- Think about a time recently when a potential customer enquired but did not do business with you. Why did you lose this business?

Customer Chat

A second way of researching about your customers is to simply have an informal chat with two or three. You could meet for coffee or simply chat over the phone. Don't assume that your customer has time to talk to you when they're in your place of business.

Choose a customer who will be honest and objective. For this reason avoid chatting to really good friends or family. Keep your chat informal so your customer feels relaxed and comfortable. This is a listening exercise, so be prepared to ask questions and then just listen. If there is a silence, give your customers time to think and process their answer. They will eventually fill the silence. Don't challenge negative feedback. It may discourage any further criticism. Remember, the goal of the exercise is to understand your customers better. If they have misconceptions about your business it's better to find out what they are. You can always deal with their mistaken views at some time in the future.

Focus Groups

A focus group is a small group of six to ten people led through an open discussion by a skilled moderator. Before running the focus group, set out clearly the objectives of the session. What do you want to achieve by running this focus group?

The moderator should be neutral and should have a clear understanding of the set objectives.

During the session people should be encouraged to discuss topics freely. The session should be between about 45 to 90 minutes in duration. Begin the session with the most important questions.

The group needs to be large enough to generate rich discussion but not so large that some participants are left out.

Customer Surveys

Conducting a customer survey is something every business can easily carry out and it can assist in profiling customers. Customers can be profiled by demographic factors such as age, sex, education level, income level, marital status, occupation, religion, average size of a family. Demographics tell you *who* your customers are. Another way to profile customers is by psychographic profiling. Psychographics explain *why* customers buy from you and takes into consideration buyers' habits, hobbies and values.

Understanding who your customers are and why they choose to do business with you can provide useful information for finding new customers. While this is a fundamental tactic of marketing in general, it is particularly useful for Facebook as you can use demographic profiling to tell Facebook who your ideal customer is (preferred audiences), create audiences in Facebook ads and use psychographic profiling to produce content on your page that resonates with your target audience.

When carrying out your survey I recommend using SurveyMonkey, a web-based survey software company. The software is free to use if you have under 10 questions and under 100 respondents. Beyond that there are monthly packages that you can select depending on your survey.

There are a number of steps I recommend following when doing your customer survey:

1. Establish what the survey's goals are. What do you want to achieve? How are you planning to use the information that you are gathering? If you wish to establish demographic and

psychographic profiles what questions should you include?

2. Use simple language avoiding jargon and industry acronyms. Respondents are more likely to abandon surveys if they don't understand the questions.

3. Closed questions, giving respondents specific choices (for example, multiple choice or yes/no) make it easier to analyses survey results.

4. Open-ended questions allow respondents to answer questions in their own words. It offers the opportunity to express opinions that you might not have factored into multiple choice answers. Although it is more difficult to analyze results from open-ended questions, they can play an important part in psychographic profiling.

5. Keep rating scale questions consistent throughout the survey to avoid confusing respondents. When creating questions with rating scales using an odd number will make data analysis easier (for example, 1 = very

dissatisfied and 5 = very satisfied). Use this rating consistently throughout the survey.

6. Order your questions in a way that is logical and that will motivate respondents to complete the survey. Begin your survey with a brief introduction. Thank respondents for completing it, explain who you are, why you are conducting the survey, how many questions there are and how long it should take to complete. Start with questions that everyone will find easy to answer and introduce harder questions later in the survey.

7. Consider whether you wish to allow respondents to remain anonymous. People may be more inclined to give negative feedback in this instance.

8. Once you have finished the survey design, it's always a good idea to pre-test it with a handful of respondents. This will show up any problems with the survey such as misinterpretation of questions or issues analyzing data.

9. Encourage responses by:

- o Emailing your customer list

- o Texting your customer list

- o Publishing a link on your Facebook page

- o Publishing a link on other social media channels

- o Posting a link to the survey on your website

- o Leaving hard copies of your survey in your place of business or at company events.

What can you hope to establish?

- Customer demographics

- How customers heard about you

- How satisfied customers are

- Gaps in your offerings

- How they booked with you

- How far in advance they have booked

- If different customer profiles have different perceptions/requirements

- What social networks your customers use

- How frequently they use social media

- Whether they have made appointments/enquiries using social media

- Whether they have visited your website.

Facebook Insights

Consult Facebook Insights to learn more about who is connecting with your page on Facebook. The insights section is found on the top administration panel on your page. Select the 'people tab' to see a breakdown of the age, gender and location of your fans. You can also get a breakdown of the people your page has reached and who have engaged (liked, commented, shared, clicked) with your posts.

Audience Insights

Once you have over 1,000 fans you can use Facebook Ads Audience Insights to learn more about the profiles of people who 'like' or 'follow' your page. Audience Insights is a tool found in Facebook Ads Manager.

Although this tool was developed to assist advertisers to target their ads more effectively, it can also be used to learn more about the profile of your fans.

Facebook Insights enables you to analyses different audiences on Facebook by:

- Age and gender
- Relationship status
- Education level
- Job title
- Other pages they have liked
- Location by country, city
- Language
- Activity on Facebook
- Devices used on Facebook.

Use the panel on the left-hand side to select an audience you wish to analyses. You can select by:

- Country

- Interest

- Connections

- Behaviors on Facebook.

In the 'by connections' dialogue box type in the name of your Facebook business page to analyses the characteristics of your fans. The only one to have this option is admin of Facebook page (so it's not possible to use this tool to analyses the fans of competitors' pages). The more fans you have the more Facebook can draw similarities in their characteristics.

Developing Buyer Personas

Buyer personas describe the individuals and groups of people who buy your products or services. They are your typical customers. A persona needs to be created for each customer group.

Use the information you have gathered as part of your primary (brainstorming, customer interviews, customer survey) and secondary (Facebook insights, audience insights, information from you internal business management tools) market research to create personas.

Give each persona a name and use a photograph which typifies this customer. Use questions like:

- Age and gender?

- Where do they live?

- Where do they work?

- What do they do to de-stress?

- Where do they shop?

- What do they read?

- What radio stations do they listen to?

- What social networks do they use?

- How can you make their lives easier?

By creating a profile of your typical customer it makes it easy to 'speak to them'. It assists with all aspects of marketing your business including writing website content, choosing appropriate images, sales pitches, ad copy, content for your Facebook page and how to publish posts that they are likely to engage with.

Four Reasons to Use Customer Personas for Facebook Marketing

Using a customer-centric approach to content marketing helps in a number of ways:

1. Your content will be more relevant to your customer. It will endear them to your brand and encourage them to do business with you as they will believe that you understand them better.

2. The posts on your page will have a higher organic reach. When your fans engage (like, comment, share, click) with a post on your page Facebook knows the content is good and shows it to more of your fans. Facebook also knows that fans who engage with your page must like your content and are therefore more likely to show them more of your future posts.

3. Posts on your page will be seen by friends of fans of your page. If a fan finds a post on a page particularly useful they may share it with their friends or tag specific ones. In this way you are reaching beyond your existing fan base.

4. You will get a better return from boosted posts. A boosted post is where you pay Facebook to show a post on your page to an audience you select. If you boost a post to your ideal customer (in our example above, to an audience that matches Rachel's persona) and the content appeals to them, they are more likely to engage with the post, like your page and share the content with their friends, thus kick starting a further organic reach.

The Customer Loyalty Ladder and Social Media

As noted earlier, customers will buy from you when *they* are ready to buy, not when *you* are ready to sell. Once you acknowledge this and identify that there are different types of customers it will change the way you approach social media.

Disinterested

These are potential customers who simply do not have a need for what you are selling at the moment. You are not on their radar. In this instance they will probably not notice your Facebook posts, page or any other marketing you carry out such as newspaper ads, road signs and so on. However, there is always that chance if they match the demographic profiling of your customers that in the future this may change.

Suspect

This is someone who is beginning to become aware of a need for what you are selling. At this stage they may notice your Facebook posts and page, but it's unlikely that they will like your page or engage with your posts. They may, however, start to notice your posts.

Prospect

A prospect has identified that they have a requirement for a product or a service you are offering. At this stage they are evaluating their options. Prospects are more likely to 'like' your page. They will potentially check out the 'about us' section and from there your website. That's why it's so important to communicate your unique selling position effectively in your company description as well as on your website. They will be interested in reviews on your page, as this is what others are saying about you. They'll also look through the most recent posts to see what's happening in your business. They may send a private message to your page to seek a quote from you or to start a conversation about a potential sale. Remember, prospects are potentially contacting your competitors too, so just because they have a requirement for what you sell doesn't mean they will convert.

Customers

Customers are prospects who have converted. There is a high likelihood that they 'like' your page and they may start engaging with your posts. The degree to which they engage is dependent on how satisfied they are with you and how relevant the content on your page is.

Advocates

Loyal customers who are extremely satisfied with your company have the potential to become 'raving fans'. They are so happy with you that they refer you to their friends, family and associates. Raving fans are extremely likely to 'like' your page and to engage with your posts. They like you so much they are very likely to share your Facebook posts, post reviews on your page and add positive comments to your posts.

When you publish a post on your Facebook page you are potentially reaching people who are disinterested, suspects, prospects, customers and advocates.

Rather than seeing Facebook as a place where you can sell, you should see it as a place where you can connect with potential customers. The aim is to consistently get your brand in front of people who are likely to have a requirement for what you are offering so that when they become a prospect they consider doing business with you.

Qualifying Audiences

Another way to think about the audiences you can reach through Facebook is to consider how 'warm' they are to your brand. The most common mistake businesses make on Facebook is that they try to sell to cold audiences. People who have never heard about your company, its products or services, even if they match the profile of your ideal customer, rarely convert.

Cold Audiences

Although these people don't know your brand, if they match the profile of your ideal customer they are likely to be interested in your content. Again, don't try to sell to cold audiences. Instead, aim to introduce them to your brand and raise awareness by creating attractive content on your page.

Encourage cold audiences to:

- Like or follow your page. Once you have them as a page like, you have the opportunity to reach them organically every time you publish a post on your page.

- Engage with the posts on your page. Encourage prospects who have liked (reacted) to one of the posts on your page to like your page by clicking the 'invite' option beside their names. Click on the link underneath the post which lists the names of the people who have liked it. Then invite people who have liked the post but are not fans of your page to become fans.

- Watch your videos. It is good to re-market (re-target) people who have watched your videos. Remember, people are more likely to watch a video if the content is relevant and helpful to them.

- Read your blogs. Getting a cold prospect to read a blog article that solves a problem or provides useful advice is a great way of introducing them to your brand.

Warm Audiences

Warm audiences are people who already know about you, your brand, products or services. They have seen your page and the posts you have published. They may have watched some of your videos or read some of your blog articles.

How 'warm' they are depends on how much your brand has impressed them.

Warm prospects are more likely to do business with you than cold prospects. Your job as a marketeer is to keep getting your brand in front of warm prospects so that when they have a requirement for what you are offering they consider doing business with you.

Targeting sales posts and ads to warmer audiences will lead to higher conversion rates.

Hot Audiences

These are existing customers who like your brand. They have had their expectations met or exceeded when they have done business with you in the past and are therefore more likely to repeat business with you in the future. The more you have exceeded their expectations the more likely they are to reengage with you and to recommend you to others.

Building a Sales Funnel using Facebook

So, you've done the research and have created your customer personas. You have identified that there are different types of customers on the loyalty ladder. In this section we are going to consider how you can marry the two. How can you use this information to start creating a winning strategy for your Facebook page?

By creating a sales funnel, you will see how you can move customers along the loyalty ladder with the ultimate aim of making them customer advocates.

There are six stages in the sales funnel.

Attract Quality Likes to Your Page

Not all likes are the same. You should only aim to attract page likes from people who have the potential to become customers. Asking people to like your page for the sake of it is of no real benefit. Similarly, running competitions or contests may only attract people who are interested in winning the prize, even if they will never have a need for you what you sell. People like this are unlikely to ever engage with your content because they aren't interested in it. Focus instead on attracting better quality likes. Use your customer personas to target people who are likely to become customers. There are a number of ways to do this:

- Set your ideal audience in your page settings (audience optimization for posts)

- Create content that will appeal to your target audience. Posts that solve a problem or offer advice will earn you trust with a cold prospect.

- Boost posts (create sponsored stories) to audiences that fit the profile of your ideal customer

- Launch campaigns to grow page likes.

Warm Them Up

Once you have attracted likes to your page that have potential to become customers, your next challenge is to warm them up. This can be done by consistently publishing content that is relevant to them and that they find useful. Solve a problem for them and you will begin to earn their trust. Respond to their comments and questions and you will start to build a relationship with them. Don't attempt to sell to them before you have warmed them up as you may risk frightening them away.

Build a Database

Encourage your likes to subscribe to your customer lists. Aim to collect email addresses or mobile numbers. Remember, you don't own your Facebook page and you can't control what will happen with it in the future or how you will communicate with your audience. But you do own your customer list. You have full control over when and how you contact your subscribers. A good way to encourage your fans to subscribe to your customer list is to offer them something of value like a free fact sheet, a free video tutorial, a discount code or a free consultation. You will find that the fans who are the most interested in your products are most likely to subscribe. You have moved them along your funnel.

Generate Leads

When you have identified your warmest prospects, you can then start to sell to them. You can email them, post on your Facebook page and target them directly with Facebook ads. Conversions can be tracked using Facebook conversion ads.

Convert

Only prospects that are 'warm' to your brand are likely to convert. Target your sales posts at your warmest fans. These are people who already like your page, have watched your videos on Facebook, have engaged with the posts on your page, have subscribed to your mailing list and have visited your website.

Delight

Create delighted customers by not just meeting their expectations but exceeding them. Delighted customers are more likely to refer new prospects to your sales funnel. Delighted customers will happily engage with the posts on your page, are more likely to share content from your page, watch your videos and attend your events. Encourage customers who are 'raving' about your brand to post a review on your Facebook page.

Chapter 12 Facebook Remarketing - A Simple Guide to Retargeting your Audience

This chapter focuses on how to get audiences who fall under the category of traffic that left your website as soon as they clicked onto it, for different reasons. There is also a category of customers who added products to their carts without making a purchase or those that only added these products to their wishlist and never returned to make a purchase. Facebook retargeting is for those that may have patronized your brand in the past but haven't visited in a while. They might also be 'cookied' traffic and those that were tagged. There are so many possibilities that make users fall under the category of retarget-able or remarket-able audience. Retargeting ads are just a way to remind them that the products they showed interest in are still available for them to buy or to tell them that your brand is still around so if they may be in need of what you have to offer, you remain at their service.

In definition, one can simply describe remarketing/retargeting as a marketing strategy that allows you to follow leads around the internet with offers that they may be interested in. This is made possible by a set of codes that are placed on pages that user visits. These codes automatically trigger your ads to follow these cookied users wherever they go. Since Facebook offers great marketing options with ad targeting, retargeting your leads on this platform is a perfect strategy for you. Research has shown that only 2% of visitors who visit your website convert in their first visit. What then happens to the remaining 98% of your page's visitors is they leave and probably would not return if you do not act fast. Remarketing tools, however, are designed to help brands reach those customers who do not convert on their first visit.

With these ads, your customers may think that the fact that they see products they might have interacted with in the past or that they might have shown mild interest in, is by a divine act of fate. It is, in fact, good that they are made to think like that as this will help them convert faster. It is also a good way to show your customers that you care about them and want to help them remember to make a purchase they failed to make because of other commitments. Research shows that of the 76% of users who abandon their cart, 26% comes back to check out with retargeting ads. These ads should be the focal point of your ad campaign strategies.

What is Facebook Remarketing?

Facebook remarketing works just like Google ads. The only difference is that these ads only appear on Facebook. On this platform, remarketing is more often referred to as 'Custom Audiences', so don't be surprised if you have never come across this term on the platform. Once a person has been 'cookied' on your website, they start to see ads on their Facebook page, relating to the interaction they have had with products on your website. For Facebook remarketing, however, there are certain features that are added to make the marketing strategy juicier than it ordinarily is. These are Customer Leads, Website Traffic, and App Activity. Remember, Facebook is a bit of perfectionist so they are always ready to make everything perfect for your business and personal experience on the platform. Let's get to know these features:

Customer List

Recall that we have explained how Facebook allows you to channel customized ads to specific customers within your sales funnel. This is perhaps one of the greatest assets the platform has to offer when it comes to advertising. By creating customer lists, Facebook adverts become more like email marketing, which gives you the chance to target particular individuals with personalized messages. This will be made possible by gathering a list of targets by their email addresses, phone numbers, and even Facebook user IDs. Also, you can make this list by getting a list of contacts from your Customer Relations Manager or anywhere you have your customer data stored. Upload this data to Facebook and according to whichever category they fall under in your sales funnel, target them with ads.

Website Traffic

You are probably more familiar with this than you are with any of the other features. This is meant to submit ads to people who have visited your site at any point in the past. Once you have set up Facebook pixels for different pages on your website, you can then set up different audiences, with filters for the pages they have visited, as a yardstick. For example, if you are selling workout kits but you want your ad to target those that are in search of waist trainers, you can create your audience to show ads to those people that visited pages on your website with the keyword, 'Trainers' in the URL.

App Activity

This is the point where you use different user behaviors to determine which ads you will show to which sets of people. This is a really good option for those that already have an established app. There are many ways to show relevant ads to different people, based on their activities within the app. For example, you could show ads to people who abandoned a certain product in their shopping cart on your app, with discounts on those products or special offers. Also, you can upsell to people who recently made a purchase on your app or maybe a person that has reached a particular level in a game (if you are marketing a game app).

Starting your Facebook Remarketing Campaign

Setting up your Facebook remarketing ads should be as easy as setting up any other type of ad in your ad campaign journey. To get started, go to your Facebook

Ads Manager account and click on the 'Tools' dropdown, then select 'Audiences'.

Once done, select 'Create Audiences' and click on the 'Custom Audience' option.

You will be led to another screen where you will see the features we talked about in the previous section. This is where you will choose the type of remarketing audience you want to create from the three options that have been described above.

Create a Customer List

To create customer list, you have to import the list of customers you may have already created by copying and pasting or by uploading a file containing emails, phone numbers, Facebook user IDs, or Mobile Advertiser IDs. There is also an option available to you by Facebook which allows you to upload your list through MailChimp's email server.

Website Traffic

You have to set Facebook Pixel on your website to enable you to target your ad with the activities of customers on your website. You can bypass this step if you have already set a custom audience pixel on your website. You only need to set pixels once, to enable you to remarket to your audience.

Once you have set your Pixel or you are sure that your Pixel is intact, go back to the 'Create a Custom Audience' section and click on 'Website Traffic'. Here, you will set all the parameters that you need the website visitor to meet before they are remarketed to. For example, if you wish to remarket to those that visited your website to search for the keyword, 'Shoes' in the URL, you can name your Audience, 'Shoe Shoppers', then create the audience. Once done, apply the custom audience to a pre-created ad set if you already have one in place, or create a new one to suit the audience you have just created.

Winning Tactics for Facebook Remarketing

When going into any Facebook campaign strategy, you have to keep in mind the need to do better than your numerous competitors as the goal is to stay on top of your game. Now that you have learned the importance of Facebook remarketing and how to set up your remarketing ads, let's now look into ways of getting the best out of these ads with these simple best practices.

Gain followers with Facebook Remarketing Lists

The number of likes on your page goes a long way to show how well your Facebook Marketing campaign is doing. Typically, people will not be as impressed by a page that merely has a few hundred likes. It only shows your audience that there isn't too much happening on your page. As you are pushing for more likes, it is, however, of utmost importance for you to get these likes organically. It is a quite dangerous practice to buy followers on Facebook. This is because you need followers who are genuinely interested in the things your page has to offer. This for engagement purposes which ultimately, will drive in more conversions. It may be difficult to grow your followers organically but at the end, there is a gain for every bit of stress you may be put through so this is definitely worth it. The good news is that Facebook allows you to run paid campaigns with the goal of getting page promotions.

Remarketing is a great way to get new likes on your page through promoted content. This is owing to the fact that this promoted content is targeted to reach your most enthusiastic fans to give you more engagement rates which will give you higher relevance scores, organic visibility, and cheaper clicks.

Facebook's Relevance Score metric dictates the amount you spend and the frequency at which your ads are shown to your target audience. The highest influencer of this metric is your engagement rate which is more likely to be higher if your ads are shown through remarketing to those that have already interacted with your brand in one way or the other. They are considered your brand's most loyal customers. This set of people can be described as your brand ambassadors because they are more likely to interact with all your posts and this will increase your relevance score. This will get you cheaper clicks and more visibility. There is also another advantage to this: using sponsored ads to remarket to your loyal followers will also get you more organic visibility. This is how: when one of your Facebook followers likes your post, that post will automatically appear on the timeline of the person's network of friends. This means that there is a potential of some people from this network of friends liking your page so the more your fans are able to see your posts to like it, the more their friends have the potential of liking your page, hence, more organic likes.

Remarket to those that are Already Following your Page

After gaining followers, you have to make sure that these followers are responsive by interacting with your page. The first tip above can be extended by remarketing to those same people who brought in more followers for you and to those that were converted, to also bring in more followers with the help of boosted posts. This tip is bound to work in your favor as it is already tested. The logic is simple; you are remarketing to those that have already interacted with your brand on the Facebook platform. Any user that has taken the step to like your page has certainly achieved a level of loyalty for your brand. This will translate to more engagement from them, which of course, will mean higher relevance scores and more organic reach.

Use Facebook Targeting Options to Layer your Custom Audiences

The number of people of different categories you can reach with Facebook's targeting options is simply mind-blowing. From the girl-next-door to the president of a first-world country, once you have a good knowledge of your audience, finding them wouldn't be a problem. Even though it is very important not to get too granular and limit your reach, it is of more importance to not overstretch your budget through a large arena of Facebook users as this will give great limits to your visibility and lead to lower relevance scores, fewer conversion rates, and even lower returns on investment.

For instance, if you are retargeting a very large audience that runs on the large side, let's say you have over a thousand contacts to remarket to, with only $150 to spare. Instead of sharing your funds in tiny sections, it will be of more effect if you combine every section of your list into a larger group, using demographic targeting to get the most valuable audience that has prospects of conversion at the end.

It is important to balance between your budgets and audience size, but it is also very important to use the layering targeting options at the top of your custom audiences to carry out experiments. This will most likely increase the relevance of your page and make sure your budget is allocated to those audiences that will most likely convert. This will certainly ensure that your resources don't fall on dry land, without yielding fruits.

Keep your Goals in Mind when Scheduling your Ads

When setting up your ads, be very careful to not bore your remarketing audience or fatigue them. Be more aggressive, however, with special offers and in cases where you have longer buying circles. Usually, the life span of Facebook ads are short-lived but instead of running your ads continuously until you run out of the budget, think of the goal you want to achieve with the ads. For example, if you are running ads for Christmas sales or special discounted offers on a particular product, run the ads aggressively for the time when the discounts or sales will be on, without running frequency caps to an audience that wouldn't convert. If on the other hand, the ad is to promote your page to site visitors, this is possibly going to be an ongoing ad set so you can change to schedule to 'from time to time' to keep your ads fresh. Remember, you can schedule your ads to run at a particular time of the day or a particular day of the week. What this means is that you should set your ad schedule with the goal of the ad as a yardstick, to get the best results out of the ad.

Use Lookalike Customers to Layer new Customers into your Custom Audience

This is a way of expanding your audience by duplicating your existing audience to get to an entirely new set of leads. This is a very strong tactic which you can use to expand your reach while finding a new, untapped audience. This is simple - this particular audience may have already converted by patronizing your brand, but you are out in search of new opportunities. What you do is to simply clone your existing in-market retargeting audience. To do this, layer lookalike audiences from the top of your custom audience. Once done, Facebook will help you find leads with similar makeup, who are very likely to be interested in the things you have to offer.

Take Advantage of the Window of Opportunity

By now, you are no longer oblivious of the fact that is not everyone who visits your landing page converts on their first visit. Now, when a person visits your page and bounces almost immediately, it is your responsibility to find out the best time which you can help them make up their minds to interact with you. Let's say, for instance, you run a beauty parlor and a person visits your page but leaves without converting. This means that the person is probably looking for a place to do her hair. Also, chances are that this same person eventually found another option and went with it. Do not take her as a lost customer, this person may still end up being your most loyal customer if you handle the relationship well. Keeping in mind that from the first visit you have already formed a relationship with her, so you are to start timing her from that time. Since she has just gotten her hair done, this means that in the next three months, she will already be in search of other options to get her hair done again because she will want to get it done again. The space between the second and third months is, however, your window of opportunity. This is the time you are expected to aggressively push in retargeting ads to her, to compel her to choose you as not just her one-time place to get her hair done, but as her one-stop shop for all her hair needs and eventually, all her beauty requirements.

To do this, there are two things you can do. First, you can create an ad and target it to all customers that have not visited your site for the past 14 days. This is a very easy option but it may not give us explicit results as the second option, which is to create two audiences: first, an audience of those that visited your site in the past 3 months and the second, an audience of those that have visited in the past 2 months. The window of opportunity for the customer you are trying to target will be in the second option while exempting the first option.

In a nutshell, Facebook remarketing should be one of the focal points of your Facebook ad campaign. The gains of this marketing strategy cannot be emphasized enough as it leads you to achieve some of the major goals of your marketing campaign, with conversion as an ultimate goal. Remember, getting ample returns on investment is very important and this can only happen when your leads convert. It is for this reason that you have to focus on convincing people who already know your brand to patronize you, by remarketing to them.

Chapter 13 How to make money using Facebook

Selling Your Product/Service Via Facebook

Once you have your Facebook page up and running, it's time to start generating your audience into customers! Remember don't hesitate to sell your service or products. You don't want to just consistently provide free value and knowledge without any return for yourself because at the end of the day you run a business. So now it's time to think of your plan of attack towards how you can sell your products and services within your business.

Getting Started

If you don't already have a website set up, you can still promote your business just via Facebook. Posting photos, videos and Stories of your business in action or the products you sell is a good way to get your customers to trust you and want to buy. At the end of the day if they have liked your page, they have an interest in what you offer and you will convert more customers than you think as long as your provide quality value that is authentic.

Driving Facebook Traffic to your Business.

If you have a product or service make sure the link to your website or the products are in your Facebook Bio as well as all your other social media accounts.

Posting

Facebook has many different kinds of posts, and they are always adding more to the roster. They will likely have at least one more on this list before the year is out.

Using Stories

Stories are a great feature that was recently built in to Facebook pages, as well as private pages. This feature allows you to share exclusive, behind the scenes footage of your business in action. It gives you a great advantage in getting customers excited about what you are offering, as well as allowing them to feel personally involved in what you are doing in your business. When people support your business, they want to feel important to you and your business. Brand experience is a great way to boost that. Through stories, you can share important moments that customers would otherwise miss. This can include fun things such as unboxing new products, sharing a live video during a customer session (with customer consent,) or even just sharing a short video of what you and your staff are doing on your days off. One great thing about Facebook stories is that you can actually add to them from Instagram. If you have a business Instagram account linked to your Facebook page, when you share stories to your Instagram account you can set them to share to Facebook as well. This means that a broader audience sees your stories and that you are nurturing both platforms at the same time.

Photographs and Videos

Using posts with photographs and videos is a great way to share your business with your audience. When it comes to selling specifically, you want to make sure that you are sharing high quality images or videos of your products and services. For example, taking a high-resolution image of your product with a beautiful background in a well-lit area is a great way to make the image more attractive, thus attracting the audience to you even more. Alternatively, sharing an image of you performing a service (with customers consent) is another great way. For example, if you are a hairdresser, you might have a co-worker take a high-quality picture of you cutting a client's hair. Then, you can share it with a caption such as, "Had so much fun cutting (customer's name)'s hair today! PS, I have a few more appointments available this weekend. Call xxx-xxx-xxxx to book!" This is a great way to show off your business through your posts and drive traffic to your business.

As you can see, selling through Facebook Is actually quite simple. You can get your customers to click on a specific link where you're selling your service or you can drive the traffic from your social media account to your website where you can then provide more value and sell them your products and services.

If not, you can simply tell your customers via private message if they're interested in the product or service you're willing to sell.

Remember by this point you would have done your customer research and your page will be up and running providing immense value. So, don't hesitate to sell your quality products.

Text Post

The original kind of Facebook post, and the most basic. A text post sparks engagement and gets your followers talking. Ask your followers questions about what they want from you and what you can do to make their lives easier, and this will get you some great engagement.

Live Video

Live video is exactly what it sounds like: a video that is live. It can be a great way to connect with your followers and give them behind the scene looks at your company, your product, or even the personality behind the brand. Just remember, anything can happen during a live broadcast, so be sure to prepare yourself well for any problems that could take place.

Linked Content

Linking content on Facebook is a very popular and very easy way to get more engagement to your own website, or other content online. Be careful to only share content to your page that is relevant to you, and that you think your followers will want to share as well. Sharing is caring, everybody!

Pinned Post

Having a pinned post is when you pin a post at the top of the page. This is great for you if you have something that you feel like needs attention, and should be the first post that your potential customers see as they click on your page. (ex. You're trying to sell tickets to a show. Your pinned post should be a review or a picture of the production.)

Facebook Affiliate Marketing

If you are new to the world of business and are looking for a great way to make money with your page, affiliate marketing may be something for you to look into. Affiliate marketing is a wonderful way to make passive income on your Facebook page simply by implementing the tools that you have learned throughout the rest of this book. In this chapter, you are going to learn how you can begin affiliate marketing so that you can make money through your Facebook page without having to sell your own products or services. You can solely rely on making income through Affiliate Marketing or you can use it as an extra income stream.

Affiliate marketing is a business model wherein the affiliate marketer (you) markets products for other businesses. This business model is one of the lowest maintenance models to exist, allowing you to build a passive income simply through having an engaged social media following. To make money using this business model, all you have to do is share products to your followers that are owned by other brands. Every time they purchase a product with your link or coupon code, you earn a commission from the company.

Creating a powerful affiliate marketing business requires you to build an engaged and loyal following on social media first. If you do not have an engaged and active following, people will not click on your link, and you simply won't make any money. As a result, it will be harder for you to get deals. This will not be a successful venture for you. However, if you take the time to build a loyal following through the regular posting advice given in this book, you will be able to make plenty of money through this business model in relatively minimal timing.

Alternatives to affiliate marketing include direct sales and network marketing. In direct sales and network marketing, however, you are bound to a single company. In affiliate marketing, you can have as many deals with as many companies as you desire. You create termed contracts with these companies that enable you to promote their products in exchange for a commission unlike in direct sales or network marketing where you become an official representative of the chosen company. That being said, affiliate marketing is a lot freer and more lucrative than direct sales or network marketing which is why I recommend it.

Finding Affiliate Marketing Deals

Getting started in affiliate marketing requires you to find deals that you can market. When you are a bigger online personality with a large number of engaged following, companies will begin to seek you out to do these deals. This is because they recognize the value of your marketing abilities and they want to take advantage of your services and access your audience through a person they trust most: you. When you get to this point, making your deals is pretty simple. However, until you are there, you need to know how to find affiliate marketing deals that will allow you to go through with them when your number of followers is smaller.

Once you have a few hundred followers, you can begin looking on websites like ClickBank or Amazon associates to receive affiliate marketing deals. These websites are based on connecting companies with marketers so that affiliate marketing deals can be made. Companies on these websites are looking for people just like you to promote them. All you have to do to get started is to create a profile, have it verified, and then begin connecting with companies who are ready to make deals with you.

When you are making your deal, make sure that you pay attention to the terms of it. You do not want to enter a deal that may be restrictive, limiting, or unfair to you. Some companies may want to make deals that do not involve cash. For example, they may give you product credit to their company in exchange for your services. This is not necessarily a bad thing, but you need to decide if it is something you are willing to accept. Knowing what you are and are not willing to accept into your deals will make it easier to finalize them, or negotiate them if need be.

Lastly, do not be too hard on yourself if you have a deal that is not exactly what you expected or if things started off somewhat slow. Staying dedicated and continuing to put the effort will pay off in the end. Your commitment is your success, so keep showing up. Before you know it, you will be earning a major passive income through your affiliate marketing deals.

Another way to find affiliate marketing deals is emailing the company and letting them know that you would be happy to sell their product through an affiliate program. They will give you a special link in which lets the company know that they are your customers who are buying their product/service. Some companies have an affiliate program you can automatically sign up to on their website also.

Posting Your Affiliate Marketing Posts

When you are posting your affiliate marketing posts, make sure that you verify the terms of your agreement with the company you are promoting for. Additionally, verify the terms of the agreement with the site you are sharing it on, and any legal requirements you may have. For example, recently, a law was passed stating that if you are using affiliate links in a blog post, you must post a disclaimer at the top of your post to let people know that you are being paid for promoting the company with your link.

Keeping yourself protected by knowing what is expected of you is the best way to ensure that a good deal does not go sour accidentally. If you want to remain professional, stay in business, keep your accounts active, and avoid potential lawsuits, staying protected by doing what is legally required of you is essential.

Aside from paying attention to your legal obligations, posting for your promotional posts with affiliate links is simple. These pointers will still apply as they are the best tools that you can use to promote on Facebook. If you are permitted to by the company, you may also consider boosting the post to increase visibility and maximize the amount of money you make through that link. Always be sure to ask first, however, as not all companies will be okay with you promoting their links through paid advertising.

Remember if you're going to sell an affiliate product make sure it relates to your business and it is something that you truly believe will benefit your customers. Quality and personal benefit are the main factors you want to consider when selling any type of product. And losing your customers trust can highly affect your business. Remember you are a quality provider only!

Facebook Shop

Well, nowadays, Facebook isn't just a place for marketing your product anymore. Now you can actually sell the product right on Facebook. Yes, you read that. Facebook now lets you have the ability to create a Facebook shop page and directly sell items to your followers.

This is another feature that is very, very new, and not very many people are taking advantage of it.

Your first thought might be "no way" but stop and think about it. Facebook is the most popular website in the world, and average users spend about 20 minutes per day on the platform. That adds up to over two hours every week. That's a lot of time.

It's also not that hard to believe, considering our own experiences with social media. We've all fallen down the rabbit hole, haven't we? Where we spend at least an hour scrolling through our feed, tapping links, and liking posts?

There's no harm in taking advantage of Facebook as a social media platform, so there's certainly no harm in using it as a selling platform. It's not a fully evolved one, with all the bells and whistles, like Etsy or eBay, but it does its job.

To do this, you're first going to need a Facebook business page. On your page, Locate the shop tab to the left and click on it. You're going to have to give Facebook information such as your tax number and your address. For payment, you can link your bank account.

After this is all done, you're ready to go! You can add a product to your shop/s.

People may see Facebook as an odd place to sell things, at least directly, but think of it's this way: you're making the time they have to wait to pay shorter, meaning they have a small window to change their mind.

Conclusion

Now that you are aware of the different details and strategies which can be used for the sake of Facebook marketing, you should be all set to implement it.

Although at first glance marketing via Facebook may appear simple, it is in fact a complicated and difficult venture. As a business, you will want to produce content to post that will increase your sales, develop a strong brand identity and cause your ideas to be spread through the share and like system.

However, this will require strong insight into the way people use Facebook and what has made previous Facebook marketing campaigns successful. You need to develop an uncanny sense to understand what 'good' content is – how to optimize your posts so that they are entertaining and interesting to your customers. Additionally, you need to know every possible trick to cultivate your popularity, using your content in a specific way to get people to willingly spread that content and increase the importance of your Facebook page. On top of this, you must master the myriad of tools that Facebook provides to make your efforts more efficient and more effective. Finally, you need to understand how all this Facebook marketing actually relates back to increase your business' success through strong brand identity and traffic generation. It is a lot to learn and can be quite daunting.

This guide will make Facebook marketing more accessible and doable for your business. By having read this book, you should be familiar with the most useful and effective Facebook strategies and techniques out there, how to go about doing them as well as appreciate the context of why these techniques are used.

The next step is to start your Facebook campaign or bolster your existing efforts. I wish you the best of luck. With a little effort and some reference to this guide you are bound to increase your level of success.

So, feel free to work upon the different details and implement them. When you are keeping an eye on the insights, it is going to help you immensely in shaping your marketing campaign in an apt manner.

Now, when you have the right knowledge and expertise in this area, you will have to implement the details. Feel free to go through the book as many times as needed because the details listed here are practical tips that are sure to guide you in an apt manner.

Facebook has become one of the most important places for the sake of carrying out marketing campaigns. It is upon you to observe the details, assimilate the points and then implement them to push your business to greater heights.

Use this book as the ultimate guide which in turn will push your business to higher rates of success. I hope you will be able to make the most out of this book and really have an effectively successful marketing campaign.

So, explore the different points and then be all set to enjoy the merits which this book has to offer. Automate the marketing efforts, put in the right budget and watch the results unfold right in front of you.

Printed by Amazon Italia Logistica S.r.l.
Torrazza Piemonte (TO), Italy

11173659R00108